Shamanism

Unlocking Shamanic Wisdom, Animal Spirit Guides, Plant Allies, Journeying Rituals, and Practices of Ancient Medicine People

Free Bonus from Silvia Hill available for limited time

Hi Spirituality Lovers!

My name is Silvia Hill, and first off, I want to THANK YOU for reading my book.

Now you have a chance to join my exclusive spirituality email list so you can get the ebooks below for free as well as the potential to get more spirituality ebooks for free! Simply click the link below to join.

P.S. Remember that it's 100% free to join the list.

~~$27~~ FREE BONUSES

- 🐾 9 Types of Spirit Guides and How to Connect to Them
- 🐾 How to Develop Your Intuition: 7 Secrets for Psychic Development and Tarot Reading
- 🐾 Tarot Reading Secrets for Love, Career, and General Messages

Access your free bonuses here
https://livetolearn.lpages.co/sh-shamanism-paperback/

Contents

Introduction

Shamanism is one of the oldest forms of religious and spiritual practices associated with tribal and indigenous societies. Shamans have the power to connect with a higher realm of consciousness than the physical world provides, and they use this power to harness the healing and protective energies of those higher realms.

Shamans do not work alone because they believe that everything and everyone in the universe is interconnected and comes from the same source or Spirit as they refer to it. Shamans do not create new energy. They harness the energies of other realms by "journeying" to these places and using the retrieved energy and often critical information and knowledge to heal and protect the physical world.

This book aims to give you a comprehensive perspective on Shamanism. It deals with everything Shamanic. The book explains everything, from who Shamans are and their philosophy to Shamanic tools, Shamanic states, Shamanic journey, plant allies, and much more. Most importantly, the language used in the book is clear, simple, and absolutely easy to understand.

Definitions, concepts, and complex and layered theories are all broken down into short, simple steps that are easy to learn and master. Moreover, numerous hands-on methods and instructions that are practically applicable in your daily life will ensure you are all set to begin the fascinating journey into the world of Shamanism with little or no questions left unanswered.

Completely devoid of complexity, the book contains rituals, ceremonies, practices, tools, tips, tricks, and suggestions on how to begin your Shamanic path and how to develop it so that you can become a powerful Shaman in your own right. Even if your ambitions are not very high, this book can help you use the ideals and principles of Shamanism in your personal life leading to a more meaningful and purposeful perspective of yourself and the world around you.

Replete with real stories of Shamans who found their true calling through dreams, visions, and messages from beyond human realms, you'll be inspired to become a Shaman by the time you complete the book. The best part of this book is that you'll not need another resource until you feel ready to move into deeper aspects of Shamanism. For a beginner, the resources in this book will be more than enough.

The book also includes an extra section at the end detailing a 2-week Shamanic schedule that you can incorporate into your daily life. So, let's begin the fascinating journey into the world of Shamanism. Turn the page and read on...

PART ONE: INTRODUCTION TO SHAMANISM

Chapter 1: Who Are the Shamans?

Historically, the oldest known form of Shamanism was believed to have originated in and around Siberia. Shamans fill many roles in tribes or communities, including a healer or medicine man (as they are referred to), a spiritual intermediary between the physical and spiritual worlds, and, very often, a wise sage whose counsel was always sought. In the local language of Siberia, Shaman loosely translates to *"the one who knows."*

History of Shamanism

The history of Shamanism is varied and rich with stories, tales, legends, and myths. As already mentioned, it is believed that Shamanism originated in Siberia. According to the many stories, members of an indigenous Siberian tribe would gather around the highly psychoactive mushroom named *fly agaric* to conduct rituals and ceremonies.

Although this "gathering around fly agaric" came to be classified and known as Shamanism, when this story spread across the world, it was seen that many cultures and tribes had similar practices. Therefore, Shamanism is one of the oldest spiritual practices conducted across various cultures and tribes worldwide, including Siberian, Native American, Indian, African, and South American belief systems.

Most importantly, it became apparent that Shamanic practices were not based on religion but on animism. This belief system teaches that everything in this world is a living being endowed with a spirit. Shamanism is often misunderstood and seen as a primitive way of living. Due to this, it has faced a lot of criticism from both religious groups and governments worldwide.

Fortunately, the idea and practice of Shamanism have withstood the onslaught of time and government and religious oppression to remain a popular practice used in multiple applications, including mental, physical, and emotional healing, dealing with the spirits of higher consciousness planes, self-improvement, and a lot more.

So, what exactly is Shamanism? It is believed to be the core idea behind the existence of life. Shamans try to forge a connection with the spiritual world, communicating through rituals and practices. Some describe this as being attuned to a higher plane of consciousness. There are many reasons to do this. One important part of being a shaman is conversing with ancestors – contacting the spirits of family who have passed on helps us understand ourselves and our world.

So, what exactly is a shaman? The most important aspect of Shamanism is that they are concerned with the welfare and goodness of the entire community they belong to. Their concern is not restricted to one individual or any privileged group or even to themselves. They care for every form of life around them, including plants, animals, people, and also the environment.

Shamans travel to the spiritual world using various techniques to achieve an ecstatic state of mind known as a trance. Some Shamans can even undergo physical changes called transformations. The techniques used to achieve this state of mind are different in different cultures and belief systems. For example, Shamans belonging to Native American tribes use deprivation techniques to achieve a trance. They fast for long periods and/or go into isolation and remain out of reach of people for long periods of time.

Shamanism in Different Cultures

Let us look at how Shamanism works in different cultures across the globe.

Siberian Shamanism

Many call Siberia the birthplace of Shamanism. Shamans were highly revered right across Siberia and Mongolia. The farming people of Siberia were said to be one the first groups to practice Shamanism. Shamans could be initiated in any of the following ways:

- By other, older Shamans.

- By undertaking solitary spiritual journeys away from the tribe to learn their mystic ways and to connect with the spiritual world and its inhabitants.

There were different kinds of Shamans depending on their specialization skills. Shamans mainly concentrate on one aspect of Shamanism, perfecting their craft in a way that can help others. This can mean physical, mental, emotional, and spiritual healing or warding off evil spirits. Yurts (portable round tents) are found all over the Siberian region wherever nomads are found and have classic symbolism in Shamanism.

Yurts rise from the earth and point up toward the heavens, connecting the physical and spiritual worlds. The smoke emanating from the center of a yurt represents the path taken by the Shaman performing a ritual toward the spiritual world.

Siberian Shamans achieve the ecstatic state of mind most commonly through the use of fly agaric. This highly poisonous mushroom can have deadly effects if taken in the wrong doses. Trained and experienced Shamans know what amount should be used and the accurate doses to administer for accurate results without any dangerous side effects. Shamans would feed this mushroom to reindeer, collect the animal's urine and consume it. Doing this avoids the poison while allowing them to achieve the psychedelic effect.

There is an interesting story that connects Santa Claus and mushroom-eating Siberian Shamans. Fly agaric mushrooms have a distinctive red and white color and, therefore, are one of the most recognized mushrooms in the world. The psychedelic effects are caused by ibotenic acid, which this mushroom is rich in.

It is believed that the red and white tunic of Santa Claus represents the similar colored splotches found on fly agaric or amanita, which was a highly valuable commodity and was considered to be as equally worthy as a reindeer, the powerful and loyal animal of that land. As mentioned earlier, drinking the urine of the animal or of a person who ingested this mushroom was a preferred and safer method of consumption of Amanitas. The ibotenic acid was filtered through the kidneys to form a compound called muscimol. This compound rendered the poison-free psychedelic effects. Reindeer loved muscimol!

It was believed that the person who consumed muscimol would begin to look like the red-and-white mushrooms which gave Santa his trademark colors. Now, to get a Shamanic perspective, a Shaman was the person who consumed muscimol, transcended the physical world, reached out to the wise spirits of the spiritual world, and returned with wisdom to be shared and given to the people. This wisdom was a gift brought by the Shaman and bestowed on every household in the tribe.

The people showed their gratitude for this gift by giving the Shaman food and drink (the root of milk and cookies left for Santa in return for his gifts). Also, the Shaman would enter the home through a hole in the roof because mounds of snow would block the main entrance. Further, the Shaman brought back lots of Fly agaric mushrooms to be distributed to the families, carrying these mushrooms in sacks.

All the elements of the story of Santa Claus and his gift-carrying trips down the chimneys of homes are found in this highly interesting practice. Therefore, some people believe that Santa Claus's story is rooted in mushroom-eating Shamans of Siberia and other parts of Northern Europe.

The Soviet Union outlawed Shamanism. But since the fall of the USSR, Shamanism has been heading toward a happy resurgence. Siberian Shamanism, which goes by the name Tengrism, is recognized today as a national religion, and nearly a quarter of Russians practice it today. Modern-day Siberian Shamanism is highly tolerant of all other religions and is mostly focused on environmentalism.

North American Shamanism

North American Shamans gain their power in various ways, including:

- Through a personal quest
- Through inheritance
- Through election
- Spiritually

North American Shamans, while diverse in skill, often specialize in energies. This can take many forms, and their work revolves around the flow of energy in your body that can obstruct or impede your energy flow. This blockage can manifest in many ways, both physically and emotionally, and North American Shamans can draw out the negative energy. These Shamans are also responsible for supporting life – manipulating the world around them to promote the wellbeing of the tribe.

Healing starts from within but can include everything around us. Interestingly, most of the Shamans there are men. But women Shamans are also found a lot, especially among the tribes in the northern parts of California.

South American Shamanism

The Shamans of South America can be found across this vast area, but most congregate around the Amazon (humankind has always made a home near sources of water and food). These Shamans differ from other groups of Shamans in that they are able to transform themselves into jaguars. Also, jaguars are not actual animals, according to South American beliefs.

It can be difficult to understand what this means for a Shaman. Many Shamans who transform into jaguars do so to undertake journeys of understanding through the physical plane, while others shed their mortal bodies to become a jaguar, wild and free. Even the word used for a Shaman in this region is similar to the word for jaguar. Interestingly, the belief in the connection between Shamans and jaguars exists among disparate tribes totally disconnected from and with little or no interaction with each other. The belief is almost universal in South America.

Most Shamans in South America use the Ayahuasca ritual to achieve a state of trance. In this ritual, they brew tea with the yage plant, which contains Dimethyltryptamine (DMT), a psychoactive substance known to render powerful psychedelic experiences. When this plant is consumed by itself, the psychoactive effects are nullified by one of our stomach enzymes. So, Shamans combine yage with another plant that contains an inhibitor that counters the effect of the stomach enzyme.

It is amazing how these people with absolutely no lessons from modern science knew how to mix the two specific plants (from among thousands of florae found in the Amazon) for the required psychedelic effects. And interestingly, if you were to ask them how they knew, they would say that "the plants themselves" told them so.

Shamans give this combined product to themselves and the seekers to connect with the spiritual world. Mescaline is a psychoactive derived from cacti. When consumed, it can initiate a trance-like effect. This is usually accompanied by drumming (or other musical instruments) to help the person more easily slip into the trance-like state. Sometimes, rattles and drums are used together.

Peruvian Shamans specifically sing a song referred to as "icaros." These songs are designed on tapestries and look like puzzles but can be read just as you can read musical notes from a music sheet. While Shamanism addresses itself differently in different cultures, this book will deal with the core traits, concepts, and practices of this fascinating global non-religious spiritual system.

Differences between Contemporary and Traditional Shamans

Contemporary Shamanism goes by the popular name, Neo-Shamanism. Traditionally, Shamans were chosen from the members of the same community. Alternatively, they could inherit the position of Shaman in their tribe from parents, grandparents, etc. Sometimes, it was a personal calling that drove people toward Shamanism in earlier times.

Contemporary Shamanism allows anyone to become a Shaman or a neo-Shaman. And yet, many new-age Shamans feel the calling to learn, master, and practice Shamanism. Many stories exist of people who said that they became Shamans because they did not choose, and they just had to respond to the strong calling.

Letitia Pereira is a classic example of someone who became a Shaman because she felt a deep calling she could not ignore. Letitia was born into a conservative Catholic family in Barcelona. She had a happy, normal childhood surrounded by people who loved and cared for her.

Her ambition was to become an engineer, and her parents supported her. She was academically exceptional and came top in all her classes, both in high school and college. She was all set to join a prestigious university in the USA. Her place was confirmed, and she was to fly off in a month's time.

But suddenly, things changed in her life and personality. She lost the happy, bubbly personality that she was known for. She barked and got angry with her loved ones and friends, often for no reason, almost always for petty reasons. She would get up in the middle of the night and start talking to invisible people. She spoke coherently and clearly.

No one could understand Letitia's change in attitude. Some people thought that she was getting arrogant because of her academic brilliance. People kept away from her. Her parents were devastated. They took her to a physician who ruled out any physical ailments. One day, a week before Letitia was due to leave, an old aunt of her mother visited them. Letitia's mother was highly surprised at seeing her old aunt, who she thought had died.

The aunt smiled at her niece and said that she was very much alive, and she and Letitia had been talking for a few days. Letitia was highly disturbed by visions that she could not find an explanation for. Letitia had found herself floating on air and meeting with people who were dead. They told her that her purpose in life was not to be an engineer but a healer. And to do that, Letitia had to contact her mother's old aunt.

The same people appeared to the aunt and told her that Letitia needed her help. The old aunt was given the strength and courage needed to make the long journey from her remote village to Barcelona. The aunt was a Shaman, and there had been many Shamans in the family before her. All the ancestor spirits were rooting for Letitia to follow this forgotten path. And that's why she seemed to behave so weirdly with others. She was struggling alone with her new knowledge.

Letitia soon understood that this was a calling she could not ignore. She had no choice but to give up her pursuit in the field of engineering and follow the path of Shamanism. She left home with her old grandaunt to learn and master the practice of Shamanism.

Like Letitia, many new-age Shamans get such a calling. However, many others choose this path for various reasons.

Another important difference between traditional and contemporary Shamans is that Shamans held ceremonial roles that were culturally more recognized in earlier times. They worked for the welfare of the tribe or community they belonged to. New-age Shamans focus mostly on personal development and the building of self-knowledge. Yet, many new-age Shamans are also involved in practicing healing rituals for seekers' welfare. They also work to heal the environment.

Another key difference is that traditional Shamans used negative emotions such as aggression and fear in their practice. Their initiation practices were physically, mentally, and emotionally difficult, and novices had to conquer fear and pain to be initiated into Shamanism. Today, however, Shamans prefer to use love over pain and fear. Older forms of Shamanism often dealt with ideas of chaos and malevolence. Today's version is focused on psychotherapeutic effects that heal gently and happily.

In traditional Shamanism, the spiritual world was seen to be the primary reality, and the physical world was an illusion. Modern-day Shamans believe that the physical world co-exists with multiple other worlds, planes, and realms of consciousness.

Some of the common elements of Shamanism that have survived the test of time include:

> • **Working in Isolation** – Like traditional Shamans, modern-day Shamans also work in isolation as they learn and master Shamanic practices.

> • **Working for a Fee** – Traditional Shamans were paid by the tribespeople collectively and individually by those who came to them for help. New-age Shamans conduct rituals for paying clients.

Roles of Contemporary Shamans

Shamans perform a range of roles, including, but not limited, to the following:

They develop deep and intimate connections with the spiritual world unseen by average human beings. They access the limitless power of the higher planes of consciousness to do various tasks such as healing and ceremonial rituals for the good of their loved ones, in particular, and the world, in general. Contemporary Shamanic healers are often divided into three categories:

- Those who come from an unbroken lineage of Shamanic healers continue to practice the traditional art of healing even today, mostly within their own community and tribe.

- Those who come from an unbroken lineage but choose to bridge the gap between traditional and contemporary Shamanism by adding, deleting, and changing rituals and practices found in conventional Shamanism to align with the accepted perspectives of the modern world.

- Those who are called upon by Spirits to serve as Shamanic healers. Such people are usually those who have been long separated from their Shamanic roots, sometimes even by generations.

Shamans also work as counselors and storytellers. They pick up stories and experiences from their outward expeditions and pass them on to this world. They are highly creative people and have the power to reach into the depths of their minds and souls to create wonderful and unimaginable pieces of art in varied forms.

They are usually far more knowledgeable and wiser than the average human being. They look at things from a wholesome perspective and can make sensible, informed decisions for everyone within their community. Many people approach Shamans for advice and counseling, even today.

To summarize, here is a small list of the answers to the question, "Who is a Shaman?" in today's context:

- A Shaman is a man or woman who has made "rendering humble service to one and all" an important life purpose in response to his or her calling.

- Shamans are not "fully enlightened" beings devoid of human feelings and desires. They are flesh and blood and have desires and needs as much as any other individual.

- Wise Shamans accept and embrace their weaknesses and factor them into their practice regimens.

- An unwise and/or greedy Shaman can be quite selfish, driving their unique abilities to naught sooner rather than later.

- Shamans can achieve an ecstatic state of mind to "journey" through the energetic realms of the cosmos.

- Shamans can also be healers, counselors, bonesetters, teachers, keepers of lore and stories, and even midwives.

- And finally, a Shaman is one "who knows" or "who understands" the way of life in its real sense.

Chapter 2: The Shamanic Philosophy

In this chapter, you'll get a general overview of the main beliefs held by followers of Shamanism. Shamans are primary keen observers, and they are not directly connected with survival and personal desires. They free up their time to observe, think, and develop ways to prevent foreseeable mishaps and prepare for the unforeseeable ones. They are basically driven to gather and accumulate as much knowledge and information as they can gather through their travels, both in the physical and spiritual worlds.

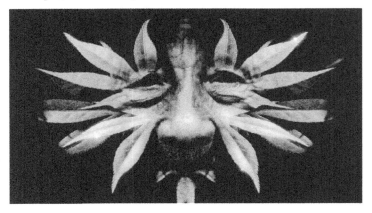

Shamanistic Perspective

Here are some of the most basic elements determining how a Shaman views the world and the cosmos.

Non-Judgmental Observation

One of the most important aspects of Shamanism is the power and discipline of non-judgmental observation. A wise Shaman observes violence, anger, deceit, harmony, dishonesty, and trust as all active components of a complex interplay of any ecosystem in the physical and all other worlds.

Shamans do not see the physical as being different from the non-physical world. There are bad, good, positive, and negative elements in all planes of existence, including the spiritual, physical, and energetic. Many spiritual belief systems believe that everything beyond the physical world is good. But Shamans do not see things in this way.

According to Shamanism, even the spiritual planes hold predators and prey, lies and truths, beauty and deception, and other good and bad elements. For example, suppose you travel to the dense, unfamiliar forests of the Amazon. In that case, you'll need a guide to help you know what is safe, what is not, what should be avoided, how to protect yourself, etc. The spiritual world should be treated as an unknown jungle fraught with dangers and holding powerful treasures.

Just as in the physical world, the sparrow is scared of the crow's evil intentions, and the crow, in turn, steers clear of an eagle. The non-physical worlds also exist in the same way. After all, the spiritual worlds are mirrored and intrinsically connected with the physical world. Therefore, one of the most important lessons for a Shaman to master is the power of discernment.

A wise Shaman will learn to respect and fear everything in the spiritual world until they learn to trust beings who walk those planes.

All metaphysical journeys and travels must be conducted with caution and wise discernment. Often, a novice Shaman works and learns from a master guide as an apprentice to prevent the harmful effects of rookie mistakes. When the novice achieves competence, they do not need to be in the master's shadows. But until then, it is recommended that advanced Shamanic practices are done under the guidance of an experienced master.

The Individual Is Sovereign

A person's sovereignty is unquestionably sacred in Shamanism, and no one has a right to infringe upon the sovereignty of another individual or being. Individual sovereignty is determined by the person concerned and is self-contained. This means that you'll only receive help from the spiritual world when you seek it. Unlike in the physical world, where sometimes help is offered to others when the need is seen, in the spiritual world, everyone walks their own path unless help is explicitly sought.

Shamanism believes in individual sovereignty because of a simple but often overlooked aspect of "giving help." Let us use an illustration to explain this. Once, a man believed he should help everyone and everything that he set his eyes on. Based on this belief, he chose to help a struggling caterpillar through the process of metamorphosis. He arrogantly thought that by helping the caterpillar, he was doing it a favor.

However, the result of this "unsought help" was not productive for the caterpillar at all. The struggle during metamorphosis gives power and beauty to the butterfly that comes out of the cocoon. When this struggle is compromised, the resultant insect becomes less beautiful and powerful than it deserves to be.

So, the butterfly that came out with the man's help could not live a full life – and died unhappily much before its time. Therefore, the man was really not helping the caterpillar as much as he was feeding his own arrogance by offering the help that was asked for. The man had no clue whatsoever about how the trials and tribulations fit into the larger plan of the universe.

Even science has a definition for this idea, and it is called the "law of unintended consequences." This law describes an apparently good decision and deliberate intervention that causes unforeseen outcomes in the future.

Shamanism is completely against this kind of help which reeks of boastful, arrogant beliefs. Shamans do not assume that they know better than a person walking their individual path of choice. And in this way, individual sovereignty is a key foundational perspective of an authentic Shaman.

Individual Privacy and Free Will Are Sacred

No person's privacy can be intruded upon for any reason whatsoever, except with their approval or at their request. The reason for intrusion could appear exceedingly vital. The person could be involved in something seemingly meaningless and trivial. Regardless of any circumstances, a Shaman will never cross the line of individual privacy without being expressly permitted to do so. Anyone who invades or enters another person's private space is not doing the right thing.

What is free will? In Shamanism, free will is defined as an individual's right to choose their own path based on those factors and situations visible to the person at that particular time. These decisions could seem to have detrimental effects on someone else. But the individual's free will to choose what they feel is right cannot be infringed upon.

Every person has an inherent right to make mistakes and learn from them. It is their path to choose, and it is their right to live with the consequences of their choices. You do not have the right to invade, exert force, or influence someone else's free will, just as no one can do the same to your free will. A true Shaman will not use their spiritual and other metaphysical powers to do this.

It is important to remember that this rule is valid for non-physical realms. This rule does not cover counseling, advice, rational intervention, and other physical actions to help people make informed choices.

Shamanism, Diseases, and Healing

The Shamanistic perspective of healing and diseases is quite different from what is seen by the physicians and doctors who practice modern medicine. And yet, many modern medical professionals advocate approaching Shamanistic healers if conventional methods are not working well. Shamans view diseases and illnesses in the following way (quite different from the perspective of modern medicine):

- Any disharmony or disquiet in the community can impact individual health.

- Similar diseases or symptoms are not formed from the same underlying energetic issue.

- Regardless of how a disease is manifested (physical, emotional, spiritual, relational, or mental), there is a significant underlying energy issue.

Shamanism recognizes five types of imbalance that lead to diseases, illnesses, and other mental, emotional, and physical problems. Understanding these imbalances allows a Shaman to take a holistic view of healing.

1. Power Loss

Power in the language of Shamanism relates to "life force," severally called prana, chi, etc. Power is also defined as the ability to transform energy which is the basis for a Shaman's ability to create changes that he, she, or the seeker wishes. There are many ways power is lost. For a start, losing our power appears to be an innate human condition, thanks to the modern way of life.

For example, if our personal boundaries are violated, we can lose our power. If we sacrifice our integrity to meet certain needs, then, in this case, we also lose a bit of our power. Another way that results in leakage of personal power is when you trap yourself in the web of your limiting beliefs. Anything that disconnects us from our divine nature can result in power loss. Whenever we do something against our authentic nature or allow others to do it, then our power is stolen for the act, resulting in a loss.

The way to realize power loss is when you lack zest for life or seem unable to gain a sense of positivity. When you find yourself unable to work on your dreams, this is a sign of power loss. Other common symptoms of power loss include depression, chronic illness, chronic and inexplicable fatigue, suicidal feelings, poor boundaries, low self-esteem, and ongoing bad luck.

2. Soul Loss

The concept of the loss of a piece of your soul is frightening but very real. Shamanism opines that when we encounter extreme trauma, a part of our soul gets left behind with that experience. The trauma could be emotional or physical. It could be a near-fatal accident in which you were involved. This phenomenon is a survival instinct allowing the rest of our souls to stay protected from the experience of that trauma.

The good thing is that the "lost" bit of the soul is not really lost. It is waiting in the unseen world for any opportunity to return to its original place. How does a person know if they have suffered soul loss? Suppose you have suffered a big trauma and have never felt the same again after the incident. In that case, you are likely experiencing soul loss. Other ways soul loss can occur include addiction, depression, post-trauma stress disorder (PTSD), deep, unresolved grief, and even coma.

3. Disconnection From Nature

Until the recent advances made in the field of technology and industry, a large part of human history depended deeply on a balanced and correct relationship with nature and the natural world. We recognized and revered the spirits in all living and nonliving things. We wittingly or unwittingly were imbibed with the energy of animistic thinking.

Despite all the urbanization and technological advancements we made, our psyche's need to remain connected with nature and her powers and beauty runs deep. Even if we have forgotten to nurture man-nature relationships, the need to be connected is not dead. So, when we get disconnected from the natural world, this unfulfilled desire creates a hole or break in our energy field, resulting in an imbalance.

Shamanism teaches us to reconnect with nature. The healing powers of Shamans are rooted in the natural world. Even those who live in a concrete urban jungle find ways to connect with and imbibe the power of nature to keep their energy flowing unbroken and whole.

4. Lineage Patterns

Many of our experiences are passed down to us through our ancestors and lineages. Shamanism deals with three types of lineages, namely:

- **Bloodlines** – This is what comes down to you through your genetic material or your DNA.

- **Milk Lines** – This comes from people who are not directly related to you but those you had a close connection with – for example: your step-parents, adoptive parents, foster parents, teachers, and important caretakers who have impacted your life significantly.

- **Light Lines** represent our spiritual lineage and come from the experiences, vows, beliefs, and influences carried forward from our previous lives.

5. Entanglement

Another form of imbalance is entanglement, which often results from loss of power or soul loss. In this case, you absorb or take on some energy that's not your own. This foreign energy can get into your system in various ways, including attachments, intrusions, and even physical possessions. Entanglement is one of the most common forms of imbalances and is often seen in many people, though not everyone is skilled enough to recognize it.

The good thing about entanglement is that it is easily fixable through Shamanic healing. Symptoms of entanglement are varied. For example, if energetic cords form an entanglement in a relationship, you could feel localized pain at the place where the energetic cords are joined. Sometimes, your aura is affected negatively by a physical possession whose energy is entangled with your own, leading to imbalances. Shamans will decouple the energy of the outside influence so that you can reclaim your sovereignty.

Some diseases or illnesses are more likely to be part of a spiritual-energetic component than others. For example, addictions, psychological diagnoses like anxiety and depression, autism, etc., are more likely to have a bigger spiritual energy component than a broken bone, viral flu, etc.

However, even physical symptoms could have significant contributions from underlying energy issues. This is especially true for premature manifestations of degenerative diseases in young adults. Often, such people get the feeling that "something is missing" or "I seem to have lost something." These "feelings" could be indicators of energetic loss, including loss of soul energy. Shamanistic healing has two distinct stages, including:

- To accurately diagnose the visible and hidden energy patterns causing the problem.

- Choreographing the energetic patterns accurately so that the problem can be resolved.

For example, Shamans may return lost energy or remove unwanted and impeding energy patterns. This part could include the recovery of lost soul parts. Shamans direct, transmute and move energy within and around the patient's body to restore harmony between the affected person, the tribe or community, and the spirit world.

The Afterlife in Shamanism

The previous chapter discussed how some people get an unavoidable calling to become Shamans. They get such a deep calling by having a near-death experience where they come into contact with the afterlife. Susan, for example, had a near-death experience when she was just six years old.

It was a prank that led to this experience. A few of her friends dared her to remain locked in an old chest kept in the attic. It belonged to her great-grandmother and had passed on to her mother. Willful and determined, Susan agreed to the dare. She got into the chest, and her friends locked it from outside.

The young kids did not know that the chest became airtight the second the lid was in place. The remaining kids went off to play and forgot all about Susan. Slowly but steadily, Susan's breathing became labored, and soon she found herself drifting into an ethereal space where people she could recognize lived.

She found her great-grandmother, who she had seen when she was just two years old. The kind lady took her around and introduced her to the others in the room. Her grandfather, who she loved very much, was there. Something in her head reminded her that he had died a couple of years ago. But they had a long conversation talking about the time he would take her to the park and play with her and her friends. He regaled her with the stories that she had already heard before. Like this, she met others too. They all seemed to have worried looks on their faces.

Her great-grandmother said, "I hope your mother finds you soon. We will wait here until you can return." Susan didn't understand anything, and she merely replied, "I don't want to go. I am happy here with you and all these people. They are so kind, except that older man there who seems to hate it here. Who is he, grandma?"

'Well, he is a very unhappy man because he was unloved by everyone when he lived. He now looks to hurt anyone who falls prey to him. Stay away from him. Don't look him in the eye.'

Susan's almost lifeless body was found after two hours when her mother realized she was missing. Her friends remembered where she was. She was rushed to the hospital and, luckily, was revived. However, her connection with the people in the afterlife remained, and she could talk and interact with them right through her life. Much later in life, Susan realized that the childhood incident had been her first indisputable calling to become a Shaman.

So, when Shamans connect with the dead from the afterlife, they see them in the form of the people they were before they died. Sometimes, they see only the outline of the dead person, and sometimes, they only feel their presence from the afterlife. In Shamanism, the afterlife is where spirits of the dead reside until they find their path forward, either to be reborn or completely liberated.

The Three Realms

All global forms of Shamanism, regardless of where they originate or are practiced, believe in the concept of the "Three Worlds" or "Three Realms." The Shamanic journey mostly covers these Three Worlds.

1. The Upper Realm

This is the realm of the Spirit (the ultimate cosmic spirit one) and the other spirits. Journeys to the Upper World are associated with ancestors, sentient beings, and spirit guides.

2. The Middle Realm

The Middle World is the observational and energetic analogy of the physical world we live in. Projections, remote viewing, visiting, and seeing are all made in the Middle Realm.

3. The Lower Realm

The Lower World is the world of raw, dynamic, potential energy. It is the place where plants, animals, and the reflections of all matter originate. Journeys to the Lower World are associated with power animals, animal guides, discussions, and conversations with forests, trees, mountains, continents, etc.

The Axis Mundi

The Axis Mundi or the World Tree is the most common analogy to the Three Worlds of Shamanism. The crown of the Axis Mundi is the Upper World, the root system is the Lower World, and the ground on which it stands is the Middle World. A Shaman uses the energetic essence of beings, individuals, and spirits in all three places to understand the relationship between the Three Worlds.

For example, suppose a Shaman needed to find fish for a meal. In that case, they could communicate with the fish's energetic essence in the Upper World and request it to appear at a particular spot in the form of the chosen fish. The Shaman can then go to that chosen location, catch the fish he had requested, give thanks, and take the fish home to be cooked for the meal. These seemingly magical and humanly unimaginable experiences and occurrences are quite common in Shamanism.

The Medicine Wheel

The Medicine Wheel is a common symbol found in nearly all forms of Shamanism. It represents and acknowledges the interconnectedness of everything in our world, including the four seasons, four winds, and four stages of life.

The Wheel also represents the unrelenting life cycle and the relationship between the visible and invisible, birth and death, the physical and spiritual worlds, and even the relationship between the routine sunset and sunrise. The Medicine Wheel is discussed in detail in the next chapter.

Understanding Animism

Animism is a concept where it is believed that all animate and inanimate objects in this cosmos possess an essence or spirit. Although the word itself was formed in the late 19th century, the idea is the core principle of many ancient religions and cultures, especially the indigenous tribal cultures. Ancient spirituality was rooted in animism and can easily be identified in the major world religions, even in the modern world.

So, what exactly defines the concept of animism? It is the idea that all things, including animals, people, natural phenomena like floods, rains, etc., and geographical features like mountains, rivers, oceans, places, etc., have a spirit or a life essence that threads and connects everything. Animism is not really defined as a religion in its own right. But it is a recurring feature in almost all religions and cultures across the globe.

Historians opine that animism is the foundation of human spirituality. In 400 BCE, the Greek polymath and philosopher, Pythagoras spoke about the connection between the divine soul and the individual soul, thereby suggesting an overarching connectedness that threads throughout the cosmos and its components.

Plato also defined the soul as having three parts, and this soul exists in people and cities. Like this, many ancient and medieval thinkers and philosophers spoke about and believed in the connection between the physical and the spiritual world, also known as the natural and supernatural realms.

The modern definition of animism was coined in 1871 by Sir Edward Burnett Tyler, who used it for the first time in his book, "The Primitive Culture," to define ancient religious practices and belief systems. Animism can be observed in nearly all major organized religions.

For example, Shintoism is an ancient Japanese religious belief system followed by over 100 million people. According to Shinto beliefs, spirits called "kami" inhabit all things in the world, a theme that forms the foundation of animism. A strong totemist tradition exists among indigenous communities in Australia. The totem is usually an animal or a plant possessing supernatural powers.

This totem is held in high reverence as a symbol or emblem of that community. Some strict rules and regulations specify how to handle the sacred totem. There are taboos regarding eating, touching, or harming it. The spirit in the totem is believed to be a living entity. However, inanimate objects are not given this status among the Australian indigenous tribes.

In contrast, the North American Inuit tribes believe that all animate and inanimate objects (living or dead) have a spirit. These people believe that the spirit is not dependent on the body of the animate or inanimate object. On the other hand, the body depends on the power of the spirit to be what it is.

So, how are animism and Shamanism related to each other? Sadly, most of the modern, urbanized world is so separated from nature and the natural world that we forget some communities and tribes exist even today that do not have this separation. As you already know, animism believes that the entire cosmos is alive with every element and component in it, regardless of its size, shape, or state, is a living thing or has a spirit in it.

Shamanism also believes in this tenet, and it is this belief that empowers them to connect with plants, animals, dead ancestors, and other spirits and take wise counsel and advice from them. Shamans' "journey" to various worlds to connect with the "spirits" of the beings. Further, a Shaman's journey is always made by their spirits while their bodies remain in the physical world.

Accepting and believing in an animistic universe is a profound, life-affirming way of Shamanism. The belief in the idea that we are not different or separate from nature or that everything is alive and filled with a living spirit helps stop our subconscious minds from hiding certain things from our conscious minds. This helps us live a more fulfilling and meaningful life than in the absence of animistic belief.

Chapter 3: The Medicine Wheel

Many cultures have tried to track the movement of the sun, planets, stars, moon, and other celestial bodies. The ancient people used these celestial bodies and their movements to measure time, and to discover, identify, and mark geographic routes using cardinal and sub-cardinal directions. They were also used to find connections between the physical and spiritual worlds.

Many ancient sites and monuments representing the movement patterns of celestial bodies are found worldwide. These monuments were used as calendars, watches to tell time, and astronomical observatories to accurately predict sunsets, sunrises, solstices, and equinoxes.

The medicine wheel is known by other names, including "Sacred Hoop" and "sacred circles." It is one of the most respected elements among the Native American people, especially among the First Nation's communities. The medicine wheel is a stone structure shaped like a bicycle wheel comprising two circular layers of rocks. The term "medicine wheel" was coined recently, although the symbol has been in existence for centuries.

The largest one currently known to exist was found in Wyoming, which is popularly known as the "Big Horn." Some experts believe that this spiritual element could date back over a million years. Among the Native Americans, the medicine wheel is used for multiple purposes, including for healing, in rituals, and even to study astronomy.

The medicine wheel symbolizes numerous natural elements and cycles, including the four cardinal directions, four different colors, namely red, black, yellow, and white, and the four elements, namely fire, air, water, earth, etc. It is also believed to symbolize the four aspects of human life, including the physical, mental, emotional, and spiritual aspects.

Medicine is the ultimate representation of the unity and interconnectedness of all life forms in this world. The wheel represents the balance that exists between natural and personal powers. A medicine wheel is an important tool used in psychology to assist patients in experiencing self-improvement, self-realization, and finding their life purpose to lead an enlightened, fulfilled life.

The teachings of the Medicinal Wheel vary from culture to culture, tribe to tribe, and community to community, even among the Native Americans. The variations are driven by each community's elders, who relate their own stories and heritage and add these to the teachings of the medicine wheel. And yet, there are some unmistakably common lessons that the wheel teaches, regardless of the tribe or community variations.

And most importantly, these common themes and lessons are very relevant in the modern world. The teachings of the medicine wheel can easily fit into the high levels of spiritual and astronomical knowledge known in the cosmos. The wheel helps to keep track of season changes, keep time, explain how to use plants and animals and their products with dignity and respect, etc.

The medicine wheel is how the world is perceived among the Australian Aborigines. It represents the process of life. It defines how nature grows, and all the elements work together. The wheel symbolizes the interconnectedness of all things and yet how we are working towards our destinies. Aboriginal people see and understand the cyclical nature of the world and the cosmos and believe that creations happen in circles.

The medicine wheel symbolizes the alignment and relentless interaction of our physical, mental, emotional, and spiritual realities. The circular shape stands for the interconnectivity of all aspects of our being, including our relationship with the natural world. The medicine wheel is often seen as a "circle of awareness" relating to the individual self from a psychological perspective. It is also a manifestation of the circle of knowledge that empowers us to live our lives aligned with our purpose and dreams.

When it comes to the medicine wheel, there are no right or wrong questions or answers. It can be seen as a personal mnemonic tool but also a symbol of celestial bodies, their movements, and their positions in the cosmos. Let us look at the most important lessons taught by the medicine wheel.

The Four Directions

The Medicinal Wheel has four quadrants of four different colors. Each quadrant represents the four cardinal directions: North, South, East, and West. The lessons start from the east (depicted in yellow) and run clockwise to the south (red color), to the west (black), and finally to the north (white color).

The Four Seasons

We are all familiar with the four seasons, and that makes it easy to apply to the medicine wheel. Spring sits in the East and is attributed to the color yellow, like the flowers that spring forth when the days start to get warmer. Red is summer like the blazing sun and sits in the South.

Fall sits in the West and is black – plants and stops are starting to wilt and die – it is time for the harvest. Winter is white like the snow, sitting in the North. White can also signify a time of rebirth, just as the world is without growth between the fall and spring.

The Four Elements

We can also add in the four elements: fire, earth, water, and air, each representing a season.

- Black symbolizes water, the essential element in our body and that which flows through all plants and animals.

- The yellow represents fire, the element that gives us light and warmth.

- White is for the air element, the unseen, life-giving breath we cannot survive without.

- Red symbolizes the earth, the element that gives us food and medicine through plants, and therefore, stands for our lifeblood.

Animals and the Medicine Wheel

Along with the four seasons, cardinal directions, and colors, the medicine wheel can be split up into four animals: buffalo, coyote, bear, and eagle.

The yellow quadrant (east) belongs to the eagle. As the messenger between God and His people, the eagle is usually seen as "above" all else, seeing the world from a higher status in the sky, closest to God. In this case, the majestic bird represents seeing the "bigger picture."

The buffalo is associated with the red quadrant. This animal is considered both a strong and endowed creature, associated with much courage and power.

Another interesting thing about buffaloes is that they are excellent protectors of their young. When a herd of buffalo is in danger, the young ones are made to form a circle in the middle, and the elders surround this circle, keeping them safe from danger. This act represents their willingness to sacrifice their lives for their young ones, one of the most unconditional forms of bond that can exist in the world.

The coyote or wolf is associated with the black quadrant. The coyote represents playfulness, adaptability, and a happy, sunny character. The wolf is intelligent with powerful instincts. It shows the importance of freedom for a happy life. Sometimes, the wolf could stand for fear and distrust.

The north or white quadrant is usually represented by the bear, an animal that symbolizes strength and confidence, as well as emotional and physical healing.

Plants and the Medicine Wheel

Smudging is an important ritual both within and outside of Shamanism. Tobacco is often used for smudging (along with sage), and tobacco is associated with the spring (as many plants are). Many cultures believe that tobacco was gifted to man in the very first stages of life in our world. Also, tobacco is offered as a gift during healing rituals and ceremonies, a token to honor the spirits and to begin conversing with the Creator.

Sage is associated with the south quadrant. Sage is used to cleanse and clear the mind before starting any ritual or ceremony by removing negative energies. The black (western) quadrant is associated with sweetgrass, whose smoke is believed to render peace and calm before important rituals and ceremonies. The northern, white quadrant is associated with cedar, which is a guardian against the evil eye. Cedar is often used to purify sweat lodges and homes.

Celestial Bodies and the Medicine Wheel

The medicine wheel is created and designed on the ground in relation to the celestial bodies in the sky. The sun rises in the east, heralding the start of a new day. The east quadrant is yellow and heralds the start of the medicine wheel. As the sun rises, new life begins.

We know the Earth as a place of life, where we live along with all other living beings in our world. So, it follows that Earth would fall into the South quadrant, the place where life is thriving. We are held between birth (spring) and death (fall). The earth is sacred to human beings and also supports and nourishes life.

The west (black) quadrant represents the moon. Only when the night is darkest does the moon shine brightest. While it might be counterintuitive, there is a second connection too. The moon has always been used to map time, and the moon dictates when the harvest comes. The stars are directly above the earth, in the north (white) quadrant. The stars mirror what is beneath them and stand for those who have passed on from Earth. As with the moon, stars have always been used as a guide. When the night is darkest, constellations of stars show the path to be taken.

The Stages of Life and the Medicine Wheel

The medicine wheel represents everything in life, and that means that it also represents life itself:

> • Growth starts in the spring, in the East quadrant. We are born into this world in innocence, and we begin to grow, to reach up toward the sky. East is the direction from where people arise or come from, representing new life emerging onto the Earth.

- The South quadrant is where the main growth takes place – this is our adolescence, the time when our bodies, minds, and souls are growing the most.

- In the West quadrant, we are fully grown – we are adults and often rearing our own children. The primary objectives of this period are nurturing and responsibilities. It represents the emotional aspect of human beings and is connected with finding our space and meaning in this life.

- The north quadrant stands for the elderly people such as grandparents, grandaunts, granduncles, etc. It also represents death. It is a place of wisdom and knowledge where the elders impart their lessons to the youngsters. The white of the north quadrant symbolizes the white hair of older human beings. It is a period of reflection and introspection and trying to understand the spiritual aspects of human life. This quadrant also stands for death.

Understanding the Different Representations of the Medicine Wheel

The first quadrant in the wheel is where we begin our life. We are babies at this stage, and our physical bodies take shape within the womb; then, we are born. We grow, learn, and slowly develop our physical faculties. Then, we move on to the second quadrant, the south quadrant, where we move into our teenage or adolescent years. This is where we spend time building our mental skills.

The next place we move to is the west, where our emotional aspect is highlighted. This quadrant represents all emotions like sadness, hurt, disappointment, etc., all of which help us build emotional resilience. The last quadrant represents our spiritual self. Even at a young age, we are likely to have been taught spiritual things. However, it is only when we grow old and mature that we begin to value the power and importance of those spiritual lessons.

This is the time when we learn to live according to the lessons that we have imbibed, and we attempt to enhance our spirituality.

So, you can see that physical, emotional, mental, and spiritual aspects are interconnected with each other, and changes in one affect the functioning of the remaining three. For example, if someone's physical health fails, their emotional, mental, and spiritual aspects are also impacted negatively. Similarly, if obstacles in their spiritual path challenge someone, then their physical, emotional, and mental states are affected.

A medicine wheel is an excellent tool for managing relationships as it represents the importance of balance in life. Balance brings harmony. When the four quadrants are balanced within themselves and with each other, the entire wheel is harmonious. Even if one part of the wheel (within each quadrant or in relation to the others) is not balanced, then the wheel becomes disharmonious. In the same way, people in relationships feel the effects of disharmony if there is ill-will or misunderstanding that topples the balance.

The physical quadrant of the medicine wheel indicates birth or new beginnings, which both bring joy and warmth just as the rising sun (the birth of a new day) rings in warmth and light into this world. Birth can also be seen as the season of spring, the season of seeds emerging with new life. In the same way, in a relationship between couples, spring represents the coming together of the partners that leads to new life.

Summer, symbolized by the south quadrant, is aligned with the adolescence stage of human life. Babies have grown into teenagers and become adults, represented by the west quadrant. Adults then become old and move into the north quadrant, representing the elders and wise people. This legacy continues as the wheel turns as the seeds are passed onto the next cycle. The seeds passed on by the elders are a manifestation of their presence in this world even after their passing. The elderly live through us and within us.

If you learn the lessons of the medicine wheel positively, you'll feel a positive impact on the way you see things and the way you lead your life. But it can also be taken with a negative connotation. For example, let us look at the four elements represented by the wheel. Fire gives the warmth and light needed for our survival.

However, if there is excessive fire, it can burn and destroy things. So, the positive aspect of fire is that it gives warmth and light, and the negative aspect is that it can also destroy and cause mayhem. The earth element holds up trees, nurtures our seeds, and provides us with grain. However, the same earth can cause destructive volcanoes, earthquakes, etc. Water is a life-giving element. However, when floods happen, then people lose property and lives. We would die without air. And yet, storms and hurricanes wreak havoc.

So, every aspect of the lessons of the medicine wheel has negative and positive effects. It is up to you as to how you want to handle the lessons taught by the medicine wheel. Again, the concept of balance comes into play here. We need a balanced amount of all four elements to survive. An unbalancing effect of any one element can topple the wheel or our lives.

Using the Medicine Wheel in Healing

As a modern Shamanic healer, you can use the medicine wheel to balance your clients' physical, emotional, mental, and spiritual well-being. Here are some tips for you.

The east quadrant represents the physical aspect of human life. It teaches us to take care of our physical health to function optimally and to our level best. It teaches us to get sufficient rest needed for the body and mind, eat nutritious foods, and ensure we remain physically active to keep our bodies fit and healthy.

Those who find it difficult to rest should seek ways to get their much-needed sleep. Those who have an issue with overeating need help to balance their intake. Those who have problems with intake need to focus on eating enough and eating the right foods. Those obsessed with their physical body and those who ignore it need to be warned about the importance of balance in everything.

You can help people overcome their food phobias, often conditioned from childhood. If people are limited by their resources, they have to be taught to plan their finances sensibly so that their basic needs are met sufficiently and correctly. Such people must be prepared to sacrifice some of their food desires to do this. You cannot overemphasize the importance of a healthy physical body to your clients.

For example, suppose someone has to choose between buying herself a nice party dress or one of those fitness tracking watches, and she has enough money for only one of the two. In that case, she should be encouraged to buy the watch and let go of the desire for the dress. The ability to make such decisions can be improved when people make informed, balance-oriented choices. The lessons of the medicine wheel teach the power of balance.

The southern aspect of the medicine wheel deals with our mental wellbeing. This quadrant teaches us to make time to indulge in things that bring us joy and happiness. For example, you can help your client discover a hobby she can pursue during her leisure. When she is very stressed, taking a few minutes off just to paint her nails, read a book, or watch her favorite show can help her regain her mental balance to feel ready to face the challenges in her life.

The western aspect of the medicine wheel deals with emotional wellbeing. The lessons of this quadrant are usually harder to learn and practice than the first two. The emotional issues that most of us struggle with are usually rooted in self-esteem, having a positive outlook, the lack of or absence of the ability to cope with stress, making adjustments, dealing with relationships, etc.

These aspects are often the most difficult to deal with because all of them are deeply encrusted into our psyche. Our limiting beliefs, our childhood conditionings, including how to manage interpersonal relationships, etc., are very difficult to break out of. For example, an introvert needs to go out and make friends more often than usual. It takes a lot of time to adjust to a new personality trait. In the same way, an extrovert needs to find a way to be comfortable with themself and not depend on society for happiness. It takes time to make these changes. But once you are aware of it, you can make the desired changes for a positive impact on your life.

The north aspect of the medicine wheel deals with the spiritual aspect of human life. You can teach your clients to delve deep into their minds and discover their authentic selves. The more one connects with one's inner self, the closer to spiritual enlightenment they will get.

The medicine wheel can help people deal with their unresolved issues from the past. It can help people deal with trauma and grief instead of depending on medications or illicit drugs. The medicine wheel teaches you that it is okay to cry and feel grief. It teaches you to look after yourself during difficult situations and come through unscathed.

The medicine wheel is the ultimate symbol of the interconnectedness of all things in this world. This fact is a powerful pointer to the assuring thought that we are not alone! And as a Shaman, teaching your clients this lesson will empower them with the strength needed to overcome challenges, difficulties, and obstacles.

Chapter 4: Shamanic Tools: From Mesa to Music

Shamanic work can be imagined as a well-choreographed dance involving the Shaman, the seeker (the one who has come to seek help from the Shaman), and the One Source (Spirit) of the entire cosmos. Shamans are required to enter or journey into the unknown, non-ordinary reality to access hidden energies, eliminate some, and transform some others to meet the seeker's needs.

As a Shaman practices their journeys between worlds, they are usually helped by a set of tools, at least in the initial period of Shamanic practice. There might (and will, if you persist diligently) come a day when these external tools become redundant, and a simple movement of your finger is enough to get your bidding done in the various worlds that you journey through.

It may be a great idea to start this chapter by talking about the most important and primary tool in a Shaman's tool kit, namely the mind. Shamans deal with the unseen world, which can only be done effectively when the mind is powerful, strong, pliable, and can deal with the dynamics of the unseen world.

The Power of the Mind

Before we explain the nature of the realms that a Shaman works with, it is imperative to know the nature, structure, and power of the human mind, the most important tool needed and used in Shamanism. The human mind is unique in the way that it is captive within our physical body and is also part of the non-linear, non-physical reality made up of spirits only. The mind that's captive to the physical body is called the inner mind, and the one linked to the spirit world is the outer mind.

Each of the inner and outer minds comprises seven separate, distinct layers. With its seven layers, the inner mind is anchored within the structure of our body, covering the physical, emotional, and energetic linear reality. The outer mind and its layers do not have a linear form or structure. They do not and cannot exist in linear physical reality. The outer minds are connected and anchored to the spirit.

The Inner Mind

The inner mind's layers are as follows:

> • **Layer 1** – This deals with the base metabolism of the body and other physical processes.

- **Layer 2** – Deep subconscious mind.

- **Layer 3** – Subconscious mind.

- **Layer 4** – Lower conscious mind.

- **Layer 5** – Higher conscious mind.

- **Layer 6** – Lower meta-conscious mind.

- **Layer 7** – Higher meta-conscious mind.

The First Inner Mind or Layer 1 is the basic layer of the mind deeply attached to the physical body. It has very little knowledge beyond the processes that maintain and sustain the physical reality of life. It is well-insulated from the spiritual realm and is very robust and strong. The elemental preconscious mind is seen in all life forms, including plants, animals, and human beings.

The primary role of the first inner mind is to preserve the functioning of the physical body. This first layer can maintain life in the physical body when the remaining layers of the inner mind are disabled; a condition medically termed *deep coma*. The first layer of the mind exists in a separate universe governed by the ego alone.

The Second Inner Mind, or Layer 2, is the deep subconscious layer that holds the species' and the genus' base inherent qualities, behaviors, and responses. It synchronously interacts with the first layer with regard to instinct and response. The second layer also communicates and interacts with Layer 3 of the Inner Mind, and in cases of extreme stress, it can also directly communicate with Layer 4.

The role of the second layer is to bring forth instinctive responses needed for the survival of the physical body itself and of the entire species. Deep-seated instinctive and situational fears and physical responses related to the survival of the species belong in this second layer.

The Third Inner Mind or Layer 3 comes just before the conscious mind level, and in psychology, this level is referred to as "the subconscious mind." It contains and deals with information dealing with species, deeply embedded racial and familial memories, social instincts, etc.

The role of this layer is to ensure the environmental and social survival of the species. It also manages the observational learning regarding other species on which this species is dependent. The third layer of the Inner Mind is far less robust and more dynamic than the previous, largely static - two layers and capable of processing and learning highly complex information.

Although the conscious mind can connect with and commune with this layer directly, it resists the direct connection because of the conscious mind's underlying fear of getting inextricably entangled with the workings of the deeper levels of the inner mind. The symptoms of a dominant third layer include:

- Lack of individual identity.

- Detachment of personality.

- Delusional and inappropriate behaviors.

The Fourth Inner Mind, or Layer 4, is the lower conscious mind and deals with the identity of the self, environment, and physical surroundings. It deals with the knowledge of societal rules and regulations, non-instinctive behaviors, attitudes, etc. The conscious mind, which is the most robust level of the human mind, often overcomes the impulses and instincts of the lower levels.

The role of the fourth level of the inner mind is to interact with other physical beings, learn physical actions and behaviors, rote learning, behaviors, and responses. This level is that of learned behaviors dealing with mostly non-automatic responses and impulses and simple, uncomplex language. It is the level of dealing with existential issues.

The Fifth Inner Mind, or Layer 5, is the level of higher consciousness. The role of this layer is concerned with gaining higher skills and knowledge than the previous layer. It deals with complex communication and is often concerned with innovation. This is the first level where the concept of justice and law (corresponding to action and consequences of the previous layer) emerges.

It is that part of the mind where we start questioning our existence. It is also the layer where self-exploration begins. It also deals with abstract concepts. This level can wittingly or unwittingly interact with the outer layers of the inner mind and the inner layers of the outer mind.

The Sixth Inner Mind, or Layer 6, is the lower meta-conscious mind. This layer can communicate with both the fifth layer and the layers above it. Most people, under normal circumstances, are not capable of accessing the sixth and seventh layers of the inner mind. Some people, especially those adept and skilled at innovation, can access the sixth layer using its powers to come up with unique and novel ideas and/or to solve problems in novel ways.

On very rare occasions, the sixth and seventh layers can merge together and operate as one. These rare scenarios represent moments of powerful intuition, premonition, and understanding something at a meta-conscious level. It is, however, possible to train yourself to access these meta-conscious levels of your mind.

The Seventh Inner Mind, or Layer 7, is the higher level of the meta-conscious mind. All the memories, experiences, and sentient events that ever happened in your mind are stored on this level. The role of this level is similar to the previous level but in a more refined and magnified way.

Solving and dealing with deep philosophical cogitations, innovations in abstract topics such as astronomy and cosmology, etc., occur at this layer. As mentioned earlier, when the sixth and seventh layers combine (in very, very rare cases), it is defined by moments of deep and powerful inspiration. This layer is where the linear physical reality meets the non-linear spiritual reality.

The seventh layer of the inner mind can interact and communicate with all the previous, lower layers. However, this can happen only in moments of absolute quiet and calm. With suitable training and diligent practice, you can access the powers of this seventh layer, which, in turn, opens up the gateway to the outer mind, a situation that's possible in near-death experiences.

A few experts are so exceptionally trained that they can access the outer mind layers through this last layer of the inner mind. These have exceptional healing capabilities and superior clairvoyance, far better than traditional psychic gifts that some of us are capable of.

The Outer Mind

The outer mind's layers are as follows:

- **Layer 1** – Individual super-conscious level.

- **Layer 2** – Familial consciousness level.

- **Layer 3** – Racial and extended familial consciousness level.

- **Layer 4** – Genotype or species consciousness level.

- **Layer 5** – The shared origin of the physical body or life (usually at a planetary or even a galaxy level).

- **Layer 6** – Galactic level of consciousness.

- **Layer 7** – The Omnipresent Universal Mind or the Mind of Life.

The layers of the other mind are similar functionally and structurally to those of the inner mind, except that instead of being bound to a physical body, they are part of an expanding non-linear reality. A person who can access the outer mind will experience the thoughts and memories of the minds of other components as if they are happening to them.

However, people with such powerful abilities are extremely rare and are rarely seen in common society. It could be that such people live alone as hermits in some deep, isolated cave in the mountains. You must have heard of yogis and yoginis living in extremely cold and harsh conditions in the Himalayas without the need for any food or clothing. These may have merged linear and non-linear realities and can use the resources from anywhere, anytime.

The First Outer Mind is the repository of all thoughts, experiences, and individual memories. It is like a timeless cache filled with all the individual's experiences. This layer is, perhaps, accessible by the meta-conscious mind, and when this happens, we call it a Deja-vu moment. When this layer interacts with the outer layers of the inner mind, spectacular forms of innovation and creativity emerge.

The Second Outer Mind is the familial layer shared by the individual and kindred spirits. Energetically bound individuals use this layer to create pathways to connect with each other. With training, this layer can interact and communicate with the fifth, sixth, and seventh layers of the inner mind.

The Third Outer Mind is formed by patterns created by and affecting all people in a particular race, and sometimes, more than one race too. This outer mind layer resonates with the third and fourth layers of the inner mind of all the involved minds in the race.

The Fourth Outer Mind is the space shared by an entire species or at least a particular genus within a species. This layer resonates with the first four layers of the inner mind.

The Fifth Outer Mind is formed by the energies of the same planetary origins, and it resonates with the higher layers of the inner mind triggering community welfare-based emotions such as conservation, altruism, and planetary consciousness. This layer continuously sends messages to the lower and higher meta-conscious layers of the inner mind, influencing planetary identity and a deep connection with all forms of life on that planet.

The Sixth Outer Mind is a galactic mind formed by the energies of all life forms within a galaxy. This layer is so vast that most non-linear minds cannot dream of even touching its edge without losing their sanity.

The Seventh Outer Mind is the Mind of Life and is formed by all life forms that are, that were, and that will be. Any consciousness that touches this layer has experienced everything in this cosmos that's left to be experienced, right from being a single-celled microbe to being caught in the inextricable web of cosmic debris.

The Mind of Life is pure spirit and encompasses the entire cosmos. It is the glue that holds everything in the universe together. With an individual mind interacting with the Mind of Life, there is a complete and irreversible blending of all levels of existence.

The power of the mind is so vast and sheer that it is easy to lose your sanity in the unending vastness. If you can access even a minute percentage of your vast mind, the journey of Shamanism will become smooth and easy. Therefore, the human mind is the most important tool in a Shaman's tool kit.

The more you work with your mind, the more powerful your Shamanistic capabilities will become. Spend a lot of time doing meditations, visualizations, mindfulness practices, etc., so that your mind is trained to listen to you – *and you alone.* The mind is what you'll need to interact and communicate with the unseen. When you become a master, the only tool you'll need is your mind. The other tangible ones discussed below become mere symbols for a master.

Mesa

A Mesa or "medicine bundle" is the quintessential tool of a Shaman. In Spanish, Mesa translates to "high plateau," which is the place that a Shaman visits to meet with the spirits. A Mesa is a "portable altar" and contains all the elements needed by the

Shaman for healing, conducting prayers and ceremonies, and for divination.

A Mesa is very personalized and differs from Shaman to Shaman. However, it almost always contains a few healing stones, totems, and artifacts that the Shaman has picked up, gifted, or earned during their Shamanic journey. The "bundle of stones" is usually collected and accumulated during the Shaman's Shamanic training and sometimes, even during their healing journey. A ceremonial ritual is conducted to connect the Mesa with the powers of an entire lineage of healing Shamans so that their healing wisdom and power are accessible in the Mesa.

A Mesa can also contain power objects and gifts that help the Shaman communicate with the spirits. These objects could help ward off evil and negative energies or even diagnose ailments and diseases. These items are usually carried around in a colored cloth bag made specifically for this purpose, or sometimes, just a favorite piece of cloth converted into a wrapping for the items. The Mesa is divided into three sections, namely:

- The field of the dark (or campo ganadero) – the elements of this section are on the left.

- The field of light or justice (or campo justiciero) – kept on the right.

- The neutral field (campo medio) – is in the middle, between the dark and light.

The stones in the Mesa are used to move and transmute energies in the seeker's auric field and physical body to achieve desired outcomes. A Shaman also carries a drum or rattle (more on these later) in the Mesa. The drum and rattle are used to achieve a trance-like state using which the Shaman can "journey" beyond the physical world and find out the root of the seeker's problem(s).

A Mesa is like a traveling altar with the power to connect the Shaman to the threads of the cosmos. The collection of sacred stones carried in the Mesa acts as a gateway to the spiritual world and an anchor to Mother Earth. The totems and power objects vibrate with their energy, and you, as a Shaman, can experience these vibrations.

Often, Shamans pick up their stones and artifacts based on their vibrational connection with these objects. When you pick up or touch an object energetically calling out to you, you are likely to feel a strong tingling sensation in your hand or body. It is as if something you have been waiting for has reached you. It is a personal and sacred experience and varies from Shaman to Shaman.

When a Shaman opens their Mesa, it represents the opening of the energy body of the Shaman. This opening act also is an initiation ritual in any ceremony. It sets the tone for the groundwork before the start of a ceremony. The Mesa also represents a journey into the organized cosmic world and the depths of the human soul, right from its conscious level to its subconscious and superconscious levels.

When you activate the Mesa, not only are you opening your energy body but also balancing your feminine and masculine aspects, a balance that forms an important foundational trait of Shamanism. This balancing offers the needed wisdom to see things in the right balance and connect with the wisdom emerging from the contents' vibrational energy.

The Mesa is a powerful representation of nature. The sacred stones connect the Shaman to Mother Earth, referred to as Pachamama among the Incas. The Mesa connects the energetic body of the Shaman to the universal energy, in general, and to the spirit world, in particular.

The Mesa offers its carrier (the Shaman) the power to hold their energy along with the energetic power of its contents and to transmute and transmit it whenever and in whatever form it is needed. Moreover, the Mesa allows the Shaman to expand the energy held in its confines, depending on the need.

How to Create Your Own Mesa

While there are multiple buying options available in the online and offline markets today, nothing gets more personal and customized than creating your own Mesa. Here are some simple steps you can use to make your own Mesa as you take your first few steps into the fascinating world of Shamanism.

Choose a suitable Mestana, a sacred cloth that will form the outer covering of your Mesa. The Mestana represents the external personality of people that the world sees and interacts with. You can choose a good altar cloth whose sacredness you have faith in. Usually, the Mestana's two sides are done in such a way as to represent the masculine and feminine aspects, the physical linear and the non-physical nonlinear parts of the cosmos.

Choose a suitable inner cloth for your Mesa, known as the Unkuna or Wachala, which represents your inner world (the view that's not seen by the world unless you choose to show it) and what lies hidden beneath the Mestana or the external personality. This inner cloth will hold the "bundle of stones" and other sacred artifacts and power objects contained in your Mesa. Additionally, each of the stones, artifacts, or objects contained in your Mesa is first wrapped in a cloth of its own before being placed in the Mesa.

Both the Unkuna and the Mestana are usually colorful and have unique characters related to the Shaman. They have eyes of protection woven on them to keep out the effects of the evil eyes. Sometimes, the Mesa is designed into four squares or quadrants representing its four chambers.

The Mesa tie, also known as the *Wrap tie*, ties the inner and outer cloths (representing your inner and outer worlds) together. Different ties have different background stories attached to them. For example, the pini is strung together with beads, each representing a prayer or blessing from the Sun, and is called an inti-watana. The Chinchero tie's key symbols are the eyes of protection that are woven on them.

Choose a bell whose sound and vibrations resonate with you. The sound of bells helps Shamans to focus and clear energetic obstacles before, during, and after a ritual. Most Shamans hold two bells and a rattle in their Mesa. One of the two bells represents the high mountain spirits and the masculine aspect of the universe, while the other bell stands for Mother Earth and the feminine aspect of the universe. The bell representing the high mountains is white, and the bell representing the earth is red.

Choose your sacred items. You can choose a range of sacred items from hand-carved stones, power objects, small figurines, cleansing items, sacred essence, etc. You must check that the sacred stones (called *q'uiyas*) are not chipped, broken, or missing any component.

The q'uiyas are embedded with energetic wisdom that a trained and experienced Shaman can read and interpret. A chipped or broken stone means some energetic information is lost, which, in turn, could lead to misinterpretations and misreading. Symbolic power objects are usually earned by the Shaman and usually form the primary Mesa item. Your Mesa bag is ready!

Drums

Drumming is one of the most common techniques used by Shamans to achieve a higher state of consciousness. The drum found in most Shaman's Mesa is a handheld instrument. When it is continuously, rhythmically, and almost monotonously played, the Shaman can achieve a highly relaxed state of consciousness, helping them reach the spiritual world. Shamans' most common rhythmic rate is between 180 and 250 beats per minute. This rate helps the Shaman achieve a non-ordinary state of mind and experience the spiritual reality.

A study was published in July 2014 entitled "Exploring Shamanic Journeying: Repetitive Drumming with Shamanic Instructions Induces Specific Subjective Experiences, but No Larger Cortisol Decrease than Instrumental Meditation Music." It showed that beating a drum at 180 beats per minute continuously for 15 minutes can induce a trance-like, dreamlike state. Also, Shamanic drumming is believed to induce synchronous brain activity, which, in turn, results in deep self-awareness.

The sound of a Shaman's drum forms an integral part of any Shamanic ritual. The Shaman often heats up the drum by holding it over the fire to get the desired pitch. The Shaman uses subtle variations of tone, subtones, and timber to communicate with the spiritual world.

How to Make Your Own Drum

You'll need the following items:

- A thick piece (between 0.75mm and 1.5mm) of raw animal hide. It is best to use the hide of a goat, deer, or elk.

- Strips of rawhide for the lacing

- Stick for the drum stick

- Water in a large container to soak the rawhide

- Soft leather or a piece of a soft cloth

- Sharp knife, a pair of sharp scissors, a small chisel, and a mallet

- Water-soluble artist's pens (for making markings)

- Plastic sheets to put on the ground to work on

As a novice, it is best to buy a strong frame for your drums instead of trying to make one on your own. Get a frame with a diameter of at least 250mm, and for this size, a depth of 50mm would be ideal.

Now, get the rawhide ready for use by soaking it in a large container filled with water, ensuring the skin is fully submerged in the water. Wait for the skin to become completely soft before trying to work with it. It usually takes anywhere between 8 and 24 hours (depending on the rawhide) for it to become pliable and soft.

Place the softened skin on a clean, flat surface, and mark out the area you want to use for your drum head. Place the frame you have bought on this space, make sure it is big enough, and ensure there are no thin parts on the skin. When you are fully satisfied with it, use the pen to mark around the frame to cut it.

The circle you draw should be bigger than the diameter of your frame because you'll have to turn the skin a little inside the frame to fix it. Once you have made the correct markings, cut it out using a pair of sharp scissors.

Use the backside of the hide (the side which was the inner part of the animal's skin) to make the markings. The outer part, which is the grainy side, will form the outside of your drum. The inner side will have small cuts and bruises (at the part where the skin was cut away from the carcass), while the outer side will look like leather.

The remaining skin can be used to make lacing strips needed to lace the drum into the frame. Remember to have thick laces. Next, you need to cut holes on the drum head for the lacings. For the design described here, you'll need an odd number of holes around the drum, equidistant from each other. Mark these holes and cut them using a hammer and chisel. Put the prepared drum head back in the water and let it soak for some more time.

When it is ready, place the hoop over it so that the extra skin is distributed equally right through the drum head. Now, use the lace strips to tie the skin to the frame through the holes. Make sure the drum head is tightened well as you lace through the frame ensuring there is absolutely no slack on the drum head.

Repeat this on the other side of the frame as well. When there is sufficient tension in the rawhide, it will have a lovely, resonant sound when it dries up. When the drum is fully ready, you can paint it, draw on it, and customize it according to your liking.

A Shaman's drum, also referred to as the Shaman's horse, is a simple but effective means of achieving controlled transcendence. Therefore, spend some quality time and effort to get the right drum for your Shamanic journey.

Rattles

Shamans commonly use rattles for various purposes. These include communicating with and calling upon ancestor spirits, allies, helpers, guides, etc., from the spiritual world. The rattle's sound can also help achieve higher states of consciousness. It is used during healing rituals to clear the energy in the surroundings. It is one of the oldest Shamanic tools used for soul retrieval and to remedy symptoms of soul loss. It is also used for divination work.

The sound of a rattle is comparable to the sound of rain and reminds us of the cleansing power of the rains. When you smell the rattle after it has been used, you can get the smell of the carbide formed when the crystals inside the leathery enclosure dash against each other and against the walls of the enclosure.

When you place the rattle close to your ears when you are shaking it, you'll feel the pressure of the wind moving inside it. The crystals and stones themselves represent the earth element. Therefore, a rattle holds the power and energy of the four basic elements within it. If you want to make your own rattle, you can use the following steps.

How to Make Your Own Rattle

First off, you must soak the rawhide overnight until it gets to a workable texture. If you use thinner hides such as those of a bear or horse, they get pliable within about 4 hours of soaking. Nearly all other hides take nearly 8 hours of soaking before they are workable.

Cut it and shape the two headpieces, and punch lacing holes at the end of each piece so that they can be sewn together. Soak the headpieces in the water again until they become soft and pliable. Place the two pieces of hide together to form the head of the rattle. Use artificial sinew to sew them together tightly. Make sure you put the sinew through each hole twice to ensure tautness.

Next, fill this headpiece with sand ensuring it is firmly pressed in until the rattle head is tightly packed with sand. Place a stick at the opening of the rattle head. Next, lace together the two ends of the sinews and the stick together to keep the head in shape, and use your hands to give the rattle head the shape you desire.

Tie a string at the outer end of the stick and hang the rattle with its head facing down so that it looks like a pendulum hanging. Leave it like this for a couple of days until the head is completely dry. When it's ready, remove the head from its hanging place and unlace the artificial sinew; remove it and the stick as well. Pour out the sand through the hole formed by the stick.

Next, put some beads, corn, or small stones into the head. Shake it vigorously until all the residual sand stuck on the walls gets attached to the corn or beads. Empty it so that the head is completely free of sand.

Next, choose the beads or other material of your choice. Put them into the rattle head. Shake it and see if the sound you hear is what you want. Make changes as you wish until you get the sound of your choice.

Now, fix the handle with glue. Alternatively, you can use some sinew to sew the neck together to firmly fix the handle. And your rattle is ready for use. If you wish, you can wrap the handle with threads or leather strips to enhance the look and feel of your rattle.

The Psychoacoustic Role of Music and Sounds

Music and repetitive sounds are excellent tools used by Shamans to raise their consciousness. Shamanic music is part of all Shamanic rituals. But it is not a performance in the usual sense of the word. The music produced by the Shaman is directed toward the spiritual world rather than for any listeners present.

Valentina Suzukei, a leading, popular, and highly revered Tuvan musicologist, says,

> *"There is a bridge on the sound waves created by Shamanic music that opens a gateway to the spiritual world. When the music is played at a particular rhythm, a tunnel opens up through which the Shaman can pass on to another*

world and commune with a being residing there. When the music stops, the bridge disappears."

Shamans are creators of powerful and unique auditory phenomena. Each Shaman has their own repertoire of sounds and accompanying rhythm to invoke various spirits. They choose the rhythm based on their need. Moreover, drumming is not restricted to a particular tempo. Often, Shamans increase or decrease the tempo, pause, or even use uneven tempo to commune with the spirits.

The music used in Shamanism is primarily to achieve some specific goals, including:

- To raise the consciousness of the Shaman to higher levels

- To help in the healing process

- To ward off negative energies that are counterproductive to the ritual and its desired outcomes

The Shaman improvises the musical sounds as he or she undertakes her Shamanic journeys depending on the experiences and encounters. The sounds they use include drumming, rattling, clapping their hands, tinkling bells, etc.

Drumming synchronizes the brain's left and right hemispheres, resulting in the integration of conscious and subconscious awareness. The subconscious mind interprets and understands information through symbols and imagery. Further, the rhythmic drumming sound synchronizes the brain's lower and frontal parts, thereby integrating nonverbal data into its interpretive capability.

Music, rhythmic beats, and singing have the power to crystalize the ability of human beings to translate a trance experience into a meaningful narrative. And finally, Shamanic trance experiences are expressed in many creative ways, including art, writing, even filming, etc. How a Shaman uses the power of sound, music, and rhythm reflects their inner environment.

Power Songs

Every Shaman has their own song, commonly called the power song. It is highly individualistic and announces the arrival of the Shaman in the spiritual world. The power song can be translated to mean this, *"I am here in your world with problems. Please help me."* The power song is normally sung at the start of a ritual and is almost always accompanied by drumming sounds.

Power songs are oral prayers that come straight from a Shaman's heart. It expresses the Shaman's personal power and authentic self. Singing the power song brings the Shaman's body and mind into resonance with the beating drum. It is always best to create your own power song because its effect is optimal when it comes straight from your heart.

The importance of a powerful song can be understood by the quote of Gregory Maskerinec, the famous author and ethnographer. He said,

> *"In the world of Shamanism, words have the power to transform substances. The medicinal or any other property of raw materials is nothing when you compare it to the power of speech and spoken words."*

Use these tips to create your own power song:

- Start your day by praying to your guiding spirits for inspiration and help to discover your power song.

- Fast throughout the day.

- Spend the whole day alone in an outdoor environment, preferably amidst nature. A place in the wilderness away from the noise of a city environment would be ideal.

- Don't push your mind to think too hard. Just go with the flow.

- Take a walk among the trees in the wilderness and open yourself to communicating with the natural elements you see around you.

- Keep a lookout for synchronicities connecting your inner world with the external surroundings. For example, you could have had a dream about a particular flower, and you see the same flower in a meadow or along the forest path. You could get a message from the sound of a bird, insect, or animal, or an animal may keep appearing to you during your walk. It is important to pay attention to such messages.

- Take on the feelings of the animal, bird, or insect you feel connected to. If it is your first attempt, you might not get the entire song immediately. Only the melody may come to you. In such cases, you'll be able to complete the lyrics in your subsequent outings.

- Once your song is ready, own it, embrace it, and make it part of your personality. The more emotion you put into it, the more power your song will get.

The tools explained in this chapter form an integral part of a Shaman's life. The more you engage with these tools, the closer their energies will reverberate with your personal power, and the more effective their use will be to you.

Chapter 5: Walking with Ancestors

Ancestors play a very important role in the Shamanic tradition. They teach, guide, and help the beginner Shaman, especially in Shamanic journeying, a quintessential Shamanic practice covered in the next part of the book.

Understanding Ancestors

Nearly all human societies tend to care for and communicate in some way or other with the dead, giving them the title of "ancestors" or those who walked this earth before them. Most ancestors can be trusted to work for your welfare because they care for the welfare of the society they once belonged to. All of us bring all the beautiful and loving things from our ancestral line, and therefore we can trust them to look out for our well-being.

In Shamanism, "helping ancestors" are spirits who lived well during their time and died in peace when their time came. There are, however, ancestors who did not lead very happy lives and could be carrying the bitterness and anger with them into the spiritual world. The energetic health of an ancestor is referenced in a handy scale measuring 1 to 10 by Daniel Foor in his book "Ancestral Medicine," using the following method:

> • Energy health scale between 7 and 10 are the "true ancestors" who have lived well, crossed over to the other side, resolved their outstanding issues, and returned to care for the welfare of their progeny and successors.

> • Energy health metrics between 4 and 6 are healthy, common ghosts and spirits (often with good intentions) but not received by the other side when they try to cross over.

> • Energy health between 1 and 3 are fragmented, troubled, potentially dangerous spirits.

Biological ancestors are vital sources of energy. Shamanism is also focused on discovering, restoring, and maintaining vital sources of energies, including those life threads continued in the ancestral line, in nature, and in the entire cosmos that make up the life of our inner self.

The trick here is not to worry about the energy health scale as much as how we create and maintain our relationships with these vital sources of energy – not having the right kind of relationship could result in devastation and despair for all, including seekers and the Shamans journeying into the three worlds on behalf of the seekers.

Biological ancestors are our bridges between our previous and present incarnations. They are bridges that can help you use the gifts you brought into this incarnation, now lying forgotten and lost, thanks to various human experiences resulting in energy and soul losses.

Our ancestors connect us to our other vital energy sources, including our totems, animal and plant guiding spirits, etc., that have been part of our family, race, gender, and community connections for millennia and are now lost for some reason or reason the other. The good thing here is that it is almost impossible to lose our connection with these vital energy sources completely, regardless of soul or energy losses. We may temporarily lose our connection with them. However, ancestors can help us get them back into our lives for our use and the use of our future generations.

We have certain irrevocable duties as living beings towards our ancestors. The most important and practical way to do our duty toward them is to give them the right place in our lives so that we can fully express our inherent purpose and live our lives in meaningful, powerful ways. Here are some pointers to help you deal with your ancestors as you connect with them during your Shamanic journeys:

The "true ancestors," or the elevated, blessed ancestors who lived well and died in peace with all their issues resolved, should be invoked as if your life depended on them. Beseech their help and request for inspiration and their positive influence in all aspects of your life and Shamanic journey.

Cook their favorite foods, create their favorite totems and crafts, and perform annual festivities and rituals. Dream about them, or with them, and get as much information about them as possible from the elders still living in your family and community. Learn about your lineage from these ancestors, and let them know that you are there to fulfill any of their desires here in the land of the living. Seek their protection from unhappy, unresolved ancestors.

For the unresolved ancestors, find ways to help them cross over to find their peace and become part of the elevated and blessed group of ancestors. Stop being afraid of them and focus on the good work they have done until now. Help them overcome the effects of unresolved issues.

Ancestor work or ancestor reverence calls for many nuanced approaches and ways of communicating with different kinds of ancestors. As you practice dealing with your ancestors, you'll learn to become more mature in your communications with them. Maturity in this realm is all about making the right kind of discernment and being smart enough not to anger the easily-angered ancestors and revere those who are wise and elevated.

Effects of Connecting with Ancestors

As you keep connecting with your ancestors, there are multiple new and hitherto untouched-upon experiences and situations that you'll encounter in your life.

Dreams, synchronicities, and coincidences – Even if you have experienced these elements before, you'll find a significant increase in the number and frequency of dreams, synchronicities, and coincidences as your ancestor connections deepen. Most of these experiences are likely to be pleasant and rewarding. For example, you could finally get something you have wanted for a long time. You could get that promotion you have been coveting for some time now. You could get an increase in income just like that. You could get prompts in your dream to call your living parents, siblings, etc. And they are likely to have thought of you.

These delightful coincidences are great to experience, and it would help you if you kept a lookout for them. However, it is also important not to be overly carried away by them. It is very easy for novices to fall into the trap of finding and identifying happy coincidences so much so that they can become so paranoid and obsessed about these experiences that they lose track of the primary purpose of connecting with ancestors.

You'll find a positive shift in your relationships with your living relatives. The world of your ancestors is like a mirror to your physical world. Whatever you do in this world will reflect on and get responses from that world. Often very old ancestors, even those separated by millennia, will reach out to you. When a connection between the living and the ancestral world occurs, all the generations in between and a multitude of unresolved issues will get corrected and fall in place, resulting in a collective healing process.

When this happens, you'll notice your living family members also making seemingly inexplicable changes in their behaviors and attitudes. This, in turn, will positively impact your relationships with them and their relationships with each other and you. There will be a paradigm shift in the way your family members interact with each other when unresolved issues are healed.

The best thing about getting benefits from ancestor connection is that your relatives need not know about your ancestor ritual and veneration practice. And lastly, remember you are not in this alone. Your ancestors are waiting to connect with you. You just need to take one step forward, and they will take five toward you.

A Simple Ritual to Connect with Ancestors

The ritual mentioned here is specifically designed for beginners. It is for those who have never made an effort to connect with their ancestors or have not honored their ancestors for a long time. This ritual aims to invite your ancestors into your life.

Before you begin, make a list of the names of all the biological ancestors that you can remember. Reach out to the living elders in the family for help. Try to go back as far back as possible, including your dead parents, grandparents, grandparents, etc. You can also include the names of people who have nurtured you and have had a significant impact on your life. You'll need the following items:

- A white candle of any type – even a scented or an electric one will suffice.

- An unsliced loaf of fresh bread

- A bottle of wine or spring water

Fast for at least an hour before the ritual. Find a quiet, undisturbed place in your home. The dining area or the kitchen are ideal places for this ritual. You can do it when everyone has gone to bed or get up a little earlier than you usually do and do it before the family gets up. You can invite any interested friend or family member to partake in the ritual.

Calm yourself and get into a relaxed frame of mind by taking a couple of deep breaths. Then, light the candle and say,

"Through the love of my family and my loved ones, I remember and revere my ancestors. I remember and revere that they breathed the same air I breathe today. I remember and revere they partook of the same bread I eat today. I remember and revere that they drank the same water (or wine) that I drink today."

Next, recite all the names of the ancestors from your list. After every name, you can say a small prayer for them. For example, say the name of the first ancestors followed by, *"May he or she be in peace,"* or *"Peace be upon him or her."*

Next, hold the bread in your hand and seek sustained nourishment from the spirits of your ancestors. You can say, *"May we always find the nourishment needed for the body to do the work that we are called upon to do."*

Next, tear a piece of bread from the loaf using your hands, and place it in front of the candle. Do not use knives or any other kind of cutting tool. Just use your hands for this part. Next, tear off small bits of the bread for yourself and other people who are present for the ritual.

Next, hold the water or wine in your hand, and pray for clarity.

"We pray for clear thoughts, clear ideas, clear words, clear purpose, and clear vision to see the path meant for us."

Pour some of the wine/water into a glass and place it beside the bread in front of the candle. Serve a drink for yourself and the others.

Eat and drink in silence and gaze at the glowing flame of the candle. Just relax and remain in the moment, imbibing the silence and solitude. Some people can see shapes when they gaze at the flame for a long time. Look out for this kind of sign that indicates the presence of your ancestors. It takes time to get them completely close to you. However, repeated efforts are bound to give you success. Remember, your ancestors are waiting to connect with you as much as you are waiting to connect with them. They just need to know how deep your desire to meet them is, and they will respond.

You can include a daily prayer for your ancestors in your regular routine. You can say the following prayers at the start of your day or just before you go to bed:

I give praise and pray to my ancestors,

To all those who came before me.

To those who want to teach and guide me,

To those who struggled yet lived their lives well and truly,

May they shower their blessings on my loved ones and me,

May they always are by my side,

Respond to my pleas when I need their help.

I give thanks to the people who brought me into this world,

I give thanks to my parents for giving me life,

I give thanks to my grandparents for the love they showered on me,

I give thanks to all those who came before me,

I give thanks to them for the lessons they left behind,

For the resources, they left for me,

I give thanks to my ancestors for being there for me.

In summary, ancestor veneration, ancestor ritual, and calling upon ancestor spirits in Shamanism are founded on the belief that these practices connect us spiritually with those who came before us. Honoring our ancestors helps us connect with our own histories and reminds us that we will remain part of the entire human web that has been formed over millennia and will continue to be expanded upon in the future. In fact, ancestor connections teach us that we are not just part of human life but are interconnected with all forms of life, including plants, animals, fungi, bacteria, insects, birds, etc.

PART TWO: SHAMANIC JOURNEYING

Chapter 6: Cleansing and Blessing the Space

The first and the most important step in Shamanic journeying is cleansing and blessing the ritual space. Shamanic journey work is an excellent tool to help people heal imbalances and misunderstandings that create stress and difficulties in their lives. The Shamanic Journey is a powerful tool to improve self-knowledge.

The Dangers of Shamanic Journeys and the Importance of Protection

The importance of protection before doing any type of spiritual journeying cannot be understated. It is not a topic to be taken lightly because it can have serious repercussions. While protection rituals are to be done regularly for spiritual hygiene, it is imperative to perform this ritual before the start of a Shamanic journey. Undertaking Shamanic journeys is not without risk.

First of all, you must not try a Shamanic journey unless you have learned the art of grounding. Without excellent grounding skills, it can get very difficult for you to restore your self-awareness and wake up from the journey. Further, spending more than a healthy amount of time in other realms or out of your body is possible. This can leave you feeling disconnected and disoriented from physical reality. It is vital to have a good, healthy balance between the spiritual and physical realms.

In Shamanic journeys, the comforting, protective boundaries between the physical and non-ordinary worlds tend to dissolve. This can affect some people negatively, making them feel extremely uncomfortable. They may experience a loss of control and feel that their existence is being threatened. If these feelings persist, despite repeated trials, it is better to stop the practice. Work on self-discovery and self-awareness paths and solve all unresolved issues in your life before trying to undertake journeys again.

Also, people with a history of psychosis and dissociation must not try Shamanic journeys. It is best to ask for the help of a trained and experienced Shaman to journey on your behalf. When we are not fully aware of our physical and mental bodies, the chances of being influenced by negative spirits and beings are extremely high. It makes us vulnerable to their harmful influences.

Protecting yourself before undertaking Shamanic journeys is, therefore, vital. Smudging is the best way to do it. It clears the sacred space from negative and evil beings and helps you remain grounded until you return safe and sound.

Protecting yourself and keeping yourself safe from difficult and unpleasant encounters on your journey is an imperative aspect of journeying. Clearing your mind, sharpening your intellect, and strengthening your spirit are key protective shields you can build for yourself before you undertake Shamanic journeys. And smudging is one of the most powerful, effective, and easy ways to cleanse, clean, clear, and seek the blessings of guides and spirits before you begin. And finally, while keeping yourself safe before undertaking the journey is important, the criticality of persistent practice taking small, baby steps toward mastery cannot be understated with regard to the ritual of the Shamanic journey.

Smudging and Its Benefits

Sacred smoke created by burning sacred and medicinal plants is one of the most common protection rituals in numerous cultures across the world. Widely known as smudging, this ceremony is used to cleanse, purify, and bless people, objects, and spaces.

Smudging is one of the most ancient methods that has been used for centuries to cleanse, purify, and get rid of evil energy to make space for healing, uplifting energy. Smudging also helps to get rid of negative and impure thoughts. It cleanses the surroundings of negative energies in a space. Four elements play a big role in the smudging process:

> 1. **The Container** – This is the holder or container in which the sacred plant is burned to create sacred smoke. Traditionally, a shell is used for this purpose because the shell represents water, another important cleansing element.

2. **The Sacred Plants** – Numerous plants can be used for smudging purposes. Four of the most common and considered sacred by many cultures across the world are sage, cedar, tobacco, and sweetgrass. They are believed to be gifts from Mother Earth.

3. **The Fire** – The fire produced when the sacred plant is lit is another important element in the smudging process.

4. **The Smoke** – And finally, the smoke emanating from the burned plant, representing the air element, is the fourth element.

The smudging process involves igniting the plant stems or leaves placed in the smudging container. The flames are gently put out, and the emanating smoke is spread all over the place so that its protective powers are absorbed by everything and everyone that needs protection. After the smudging process is completed, the ashes are returned to Mother Earth.

Benefits of Smudging

Smudging purifies and cleanses not only negative energy but also harmful bacteria, viruses, and fungi, ensuring your ritual space is cleansed physically, emotionally, and spiritually. Smudging improves the power to connect with the spiritual realm.

The healing effect of the smoke is known to calm and cleanse the mind of the Shamanic healer to resolve and reflect on dilemmas and help seekers solve their problems. The smudging process's relaxing effects help the Shaman focus on their impending journey.

Further, some sacred plants, such as sage, contain thujone, a mildly psychoactive substance that helps take the Shaman into a heightened state of consciousness. Also, it elevates the mood, thereby banishing negativity.

Also, how this happens is even explained by modern science. Smudging removes positive ions accumulated in the environment, a natural antidepressant process. The smoke from smudging changes the molecular structure of the air and the surrounding environment resulting in a cleaner and purer energy and environment than before.

The fragrance from the smoke has an uplifting, divine aroma that naturally refreshes and rejuvenates the surrounding environment. The lingering fragrance helps to combat fear, grief, pain, anxieties, etc. Shamans recall this fragrance whenever they feel fear or anxiety during their Shamanic journey.

Tips and Tricks for Smudging

Let us begin this section by teaching you how to perform smudging. As mentioned earlier, many herbs can be used for this purpose (different herbs and their properties are discussed later on in this chapter). For starters, you can use sage.

Materials needed:

> • Sage stick (you can use an herb bundle or any other smudge stick)

> • Matches or candles to light the sage

> • A fireproof smudging bowl. Traditionalists use an abalone shell for this purpose. However, it is okay to use any bowl as long as it is fire-resistant. Preferably, use a new, unused bowl and keep it for the purpose of rituals only. Do not take the bowl back to the kitchen for other routine uses.

> • A pot of sand to bury the ashes after completing the smudging process

Once the materials are ready, use the following steps for the smudging ritual:

Step 1 – First, set an intention. What is your desired outcome from the smudging ritual? Smudging could be asking for protection for the home or the ritual space. As we are talking about smudging before undertaking a Shamanic journey, we will use an illustrative intention for this purpose.

You can say,

> *"Protect this space from evil and negative forces and energies. Keep me safe from harmful beings that I might encounter during my journey. Empower me with discerning powers so that I can distinguish those with harmful intent from those with good intent. Bring me back safe from my journeys. And guide me to find the answers I am looking for."*

Some people refer to this as a smudging prayer.

Take a moment to meditate on this prayer. Repeat it a couple of times.

Step 2 – Open all doors and windows. If you are performing the journeying ritual in an enclosed space, then during the smudging process, open the doors and windows so that the negative forces can be directed out of your space by the purifying, blessing smoke. If you are doing the ritual in an open space, then draw a ritual circle and direct the negative energies outside the circle.

Step 3 – Ignite the sage stick or herb bundle. Ensure you hold the stick over the bowl so that the ash that's formed while igniting it falls into the bowl. Use your matches or candle to light the end of the smudge stick. When the flames ignite, gently blow on them until the flames are extinguished. When you do this, healing smoke will be released by the smudge stick.

Step 4 – With the smoking stick in your hand (held over the bowl), walk around the ritual space, repeating your intention ensuring all the things, every nook and corner, and all the people present are swathed in the healing, protective smoke. Take care not to send off billowing balls of smoke toward anyone or anything, lest something disastrous happens. Even a small amount of smoke has a great cleansing, purifying effect. If, for some reason, the smoke goes out, relight the stick and continue the smudging process until the entire space is cleansed, purified, and blessed.

Step 5 - Smudging in the Seven Directions - Smudging in the following seven directions ensures your protective cage keeps you safe from all sides. Here's how you go about it:

- **Face East** - Hold the smoking smudge stick towards the east and say the following prayer, *"The energy of the beginning, the power of the rising sun, the light of early illumination, the energies of the east, protect us from all evil."*

- **Face South** - Turn southward, extend the stick to the south, and repeat this prayer, *"The energy of ancestral service, the power of action and healing, the heat of the noon, the powers of the south, protect this ritual and all the people involved in it."*

- **Face West** - Next, turn toward the west, and repeat this prayer, *"The power of gift-giving, the energy of renewal and revival, the energies of the west, give us protection."*

- **Face North** - Next, turn northward and say this prayer, *"The powers of wisdom and experience, the energies of my ancestors, the spirits of the north, grant us wisdom and protection."*

- **Look up Towards the Sky** - Hold the smudge above you, pointing toward the sky, and say, *"The spirits of the sky, space, and the Above, the star people, cloud people, and the Father Sky, the energies of all things masculine, the energy that balances and strengthens the masculine, grant us strength and protection."*

- **Look Down toward the Ground** - Kneel, touch the ground, and say, *"The powers of Mother Earth, the energies of all things feminine, the energy that balances the* *masculine, the spirits of all things below, give us your protection."*

• **Close Your Eyes and Look within You** – Hold your hand over your heart and say, *"The powers of Within, the strength that lies inside me, the energy that connects me to the divine and the world around me, grant us wisdom, strength, and protection."*

Step 6 – Put the smoking stick in the bowl and keep it in a safe place as the smoke will continue for a while. Keeping the smudging smoke on until you return from the Shamanic journey may be useful. Experienced Shamans who spend long hours (sometimes even days) on their journeys make sure one or two people in the group take the responsibility of keeping the smudging going.

A word of warning is to make sure the stick is not left unattended without taking due care. Make sure the bowl is big enough to hold the smudging bundle fully inside it ensuring there is no avoidable harm from the smoke. When the ritual is over, transfer the residual ashes into the pot of sand. Alternatively, you can bury the ashes under the earth.

Herbs for Smudging

As already mentioned, multiple herbs are available for the purpose of smudging. The most commonly and traditionally used ones are sage, cedar, and sandalwood. Let us look at a few herbs used for smudging and their properties.

• **Sage**

The most important use of sage is for healing. Smudging with sage blesses, cleanses, and heals the person and targeted objects. This herb is used to clear and dissolve the boundaries between worlds. It helps to "wash off" the effects of the physical world from Shamans intending to undertake Shamanic journeys.

Sage helps to get rid of unwanted energies from people, objects, and the surroundings. Sage comes from a variety of Geni. The true sages come from the Salvia genus and are effective and offer strong healing and protective powers. Two of the most excellent sage varieties used for rituals are Salvia Apiana (or white sage) and Salvia Officinalis (or garden sage). White sage is also called Sacred Sage or California White Sage.

• Cedar

Cedar is an excellent healing herb. The spirits of cedar trees are like the trees themselves; old, wise, and powerful. These trees and their spirits have seen and experienced a lot of things throughout their lifetimes, and thanks to this experience, they have the power not only to heal but also to discern between the good and bad. Cedar is the herb of choice to get rid of unwanted influences.

Like sage, there are multiple varieties of cedar. The ones that work well in protection and healing rituals are Thuja, Cedrus, Juniperus, and Libdocedrus. Although technically, junipers are not cedars, they are used by many practitioners for smudging.

- **Sweetgrass**

This herb goes by other names, including vanilla grass, holy grass, and Seneca grass. With its distinctively sweet, vanilla-like odor, sweetgrass holds the breath of Mother Earth, delivering us her limitless love. Sweetgrass smudging reminds us of the power and essence of all things feminine and also the irrefutable fact that Mother Earth provides well for all our needs.

In addition to using dried sweetgrass in your smudging bundle, you can also cut up fresh sweetgrass onto a bed of hot charcoal to get the desired effects. You can pass the object that needs to be blessed, cleansed, and protected over the smoke emanating from the sweetgrass-powered charcoal. Also, you can use a smudging feather to spread the smoke all over the surrounding environment.

- Lavender

Lavender is often used to invoke and invite spirits to attend rituals and also to safeguard against negative and evil forces. In ancient Egypt, this herb was essential for the mummification process. Christians also believe that the clothes of Baby Jesus were spread on a lavender bush from where the garments got their fragrance.

- Frankincense

This herb was used to embalm the bodies of Egyptian Pharaohs. This tree resin is believed to protect and cleanse the soul. The smoke of Frankincense is believed to increase the powers of clairvoyance.

- Myrrh

Myrrh and Frankincense were once considered to be more valuable than gold. The smoke of Myrrh is believed to help to maintain the state of enlightenment. Myrrh is also used to connect you with the spirit of youth. It is known to clear the path leading to your truth of debris.

• Copal

Copal is a tree sap native to Mexico and is considered to be the blood of trees. You can smell a citrus-like, sharp, clean, and crisp aroma when it is burned. For many Mexican tribes, copal is considered to be a "pleasing gift" for their gods.

A smudging feather is used to brush smudging smoke over the object, person, or the surrounding space. Remember to use the underside of the feather to do this because this is the side that faces Mother Earth when the bird is flying.

While many scientific names have been used in this section (and it is really good to know them), you must remember that from a Shamanic ritual perspective, these names do not matter to the traditional practitioner. All experienced Shamans know and sense the power and energies held in healing and protective herbs. Here are some more herbs used for cleansing and clearing purposes:

Aspen is used for protection. The essential oils from its leaves help to reduce anxiety. Since aspen burns quickly, many practitioners prefer to add the oil to sage or any other smudge spray.

Rosemary is soothing, relaxing, and promotes a deep sense of peace. It removes negative energy from the surroundings and is often included in sage smudging bundles.

Lemongrass's purifying and cleansing actions also render energizing effects. It is excellent to enhance focus and clarity. **Cinnamon** increases energy, heals, and brings prosperity and good fortune. **Blue Spruce** is a rare herb, and yet, like cedar, it is commonly used for smudging purposes. It renders grace, nobility, and serenity to people imbibing its smoke.

Eucalyptus is excellent for boosting energy and cleansing. **Clove** is often used to increase psychic powers and to produce spiritual vibrations. **Dandelion**, associated with the air element, is used by practitioners for spirit calling and divination.

You can combine any of the herbs mentioned above to customize your smudging bundle for specific needs.

How to Create Your Own Smudging Bundle

The materials needed to make your own smudging bundle are:

- 10-15 sprigs each of various herbs, according to your choice and need. Sage is included in most smudge bundles. Limit the number to less than 5. Sometimes, overloading a smudging bundle with too many varieties can mean ending up with a bundle filled with herbs whose effects counter one another.

- Twine.

- Scissors.

Start the process by trimming the flowers, stems, roots, and herbs to a more or less uniform size. Create a nice bundle that's easy to hold. Take a piece of twine and tie the bundle together, starting from one end. Wrap the twine along the length of the bundle until you reach the other end.

Make sure you wrap the bundle tightly enough to maintain its shape even after the bundle dries up. Secure the ends of the twine with a tight knot. If you see any stems or leaves sticking out of the bundle, snip them off. The rest is easy. Simply leave this bundle under the sun (in a safe, undisturbed location) for about two weeks until it is completely dry.

To reiterate, you must protect yourself, the ritual space, and other stakeholders from the potential dangers of Shamanic journeys. Practice persistently and keep building your skills.

Chapter 7: Getting into the Shamanic State of Consciousness

Let us begin this chapter by teaching you about the states of consciousness of the human mind. Psychologically speaking, consciousness describes your awareness of your mental and physical experiences. Not all forms of consciousness are the same, as there are multiple levels and different states of consciousness. Further, numerous factors impact these states of awareness in different ways.

Interestingly, human consciousness is compared to a stream that's constantly and dynamically changing yet smooth flowing. Your mind moves from one thought to another effortlessly, even if consecutive thoughts are drastically different from each other. For example, you could be thinking about your dog at one moment, and in the next instant, you could be thinking of a book you read many years ago. This shift between thoughts is effortless and automatic.

Human consciousness is deeply interconnected with levels of awareness. For example, if you are feeling sleepy or drowsy, your level of awareness will be low. On the contrary, taking a stimulant is likely to heighten your level of awareness. When your awareness is at a low level, although you seem to be unaware of all the happenings in your surroundings, your brain can still absorb and process all the signals it receives.

For example, have you automatically grabbed a blanket whenever you felt cold, even when you are fast asleep? That happens because your brain is still processing and responding to information and signals it is receiving. So, even though your conscious mind is not aware of feeling cold, the brain receives a signal and drives your subconscious or mind to reach out for a blanket.

When you have a heightened sense of awareness, you control your thoughts more than when your awareness level is low. In this scenario, your ability to pay attention to details and analyze everything happening around you is very high. This level of heightened awareness only occurs during certain states of consciousness. Multiple factors affect consciousness.

- **Sleep**

Even when we sleep, our brains are active and continue receiving and responding to signals. The study of sleep has fascinated scientists for a long time now, and the availability of advanced technologies has paved the way for the study of sleep in unprecedented ways. Reduced and compromised sleep duration and quality impacts levels of awareness significantly, which, in turn, affects the states of consciousness.

- **Body Clock**

- Our body clock is called the circadian rhythm and is different for different people. Some people are highly energetic in the morning, and their energy level wanes slowly. Their energy levels are very low by the evening.

- For others, energy levels fluctuate in the opposite direction. They are sleepy and drowsy in the morning and feel peppy and active as evening and night approach. The circadian rhythm plays a very important role in human consciousness because these rhythms determine our level of awareness or alertness. Therefore, Shamans use intense fasting and sleep deprivation to achieve altered states of consciousness.

- **Hypnosis**

- A person under hypnosis appears as if they are asleep when, in fact, the person is processing thoughts through a focused, deep level of awareness. Hypnosis affects states of consciousness in varying ways, and Shamans use this option to achieve a Shamanic state of consciousness.

- **Dreams**

- These are lucid dreams or dreams that you can recall vividly when you wake up to happen during REM (rapid eye movement) sleep. During REM sleep, the level of brain activity is the same as when you are awake. However, your level of awareness is low. It is now known that our ability to dream is connected with our consciousness.

- **Drugs**

Stimulants, depressants, and hallucinogens impact states of consciousness in different ways and at different intensities. Stimulants heighten awareness levels, often leading to feelings of euphoria. Depressants reduce awareness and are used to reduce stress and increase relaxation and calmness. Hallucinogens bring about an altered sense of reality and can lead to feelings of paranoia.

Shamanic Trance

So, what is the Shamanic state of consciousness or the Shamanic trance? Let us try and explain it. We use multiple methods to understand ourselves and the world around us, including delving deep into ourselves and expanding wide into space. We also project parts of ourselves, either outward or inward, for this purpose. The deeper we delve inward, the more we understand ourselves and the world around us. At the level of the soul, the self is, perhaps, in the most authentic form.

When we project ourselves outward, we seek to understand our relationships with others. These parts of we also appear in dreams as images. In all these deep-diving and expanding forms of self-awareness, images and visuals are used to understand our experiences. The self at the level of the soul seeks to reveal and integrate all our inner and outer experiences into something wholesome and cohesive.

All these experiences are already happening for most of us. However, very few of us are consciously aware of these deep-level experiences. They happen subconsciously. Our dreams are merely fragments of these, many of which we cannot make sense of. We live our lives without guidance despite having help well within our reach.

When we become intensely conscious and aware of all our experiences at all levels of awareness, we can begin to perceive clear, unmistakable patterns that can potentially lead us to what is known as our "truth." The deliberate effort taken to see these patterns by enhancing our sense and level of awareness is called the Shamanic journey, and the state of consciousness is called the Shamanic state of consciousness or the Shamanic trance. The Shamanic Journey is undertaken when the consciousness is in an altered state. The Shamanic trance is achieved through various methods, which are discussed later on in this chapter.

Multiple studies have revealed that the Shamanic trance is real, and the experiences during this time can help open hidden layers in our understanding which, in turn, helps us see things in a new light. A research article titled "Neural Correlates of the Shamanic State of Consciousness," published in March 2021, discussed the outcomes of a neural study done on 24 Shamanic practitioners and 24 non-Shamanic controls.

Assessments were made on various brain-related neural factors that were impacted in these volunteers during rest while listening to classical music and Shamanic drumming. It was noticed that reactions in the brains of Shamans were significantly different from those of the non-Shaman individuals under the influence of psychedelics. Shamans showed increased gamma power which coincides with elementary visual alterations. This and other findings in this study demonstrated that Shamanic trances are distinct states of consciousness.

Similar observations were made in a research article entitled "Brain changes during a Shamanic trance: Altered modes of consciousness, hemispheric laterality, and systemic psychobiology," published in December 2016 in Cogent Psychology. Therefore, Shamanic trance happens, and the significantly heightened state of consciousness achieved can help the Shaman connect to and communicate with beings beyond the human world.

When a Shaman is in a trance, they bridge the gap between the waking and sleeping world. They can move between the levels of this space, including the many levels of the human mind, to gain a better understanding of themselves and all around them. If ever you have caught yourself daydreaming, you have touched the very first state of a Shamanic trance.

Levels of Shamanic Trance

Five levels of Shamanic trance can be achieved: a very light trance, light trance, medium trance, deep trance, and a very deep trance. Let us give a bit in detail at each of these levels.

1. Very Light Trance

This is the very first level of trance and involves enhancing the awareness of your inner workings. At this level, you become increasingly conscious of your thoughts, the physical sensations you may feel, and your emotions – people who diligently practice mindfulness experience this level of very light trance frequently.

2. Light Trance

When you daydream, you are in a light trance. You do not notice your surroundings anymore; you do not notice your heartbeat or your breathing; you have left the physical space for a moment. This can happen when you are engaged in an activity – reading a book or driving your car. It feels like your body is on autopilot while your mind is elsewhere.

3. Medium Trance

A person at the medium trance level feels as if they are "in the zone." Being "in the zone" is also referred to as the "flow state." Not only do you lose focus on your own body, your breathing, and spatial awareness, but you can lose your sense of time too.

4. Deep Trance

Although we most often delve into this state through deep sleep, it can be achieved when awake too. It is a balance between the state we are in when asleep and our awareness right before.

You'll have experienced this many times during your life. For example, if you have laid down for a nap and have experienced a dreamy, trance-like state where sounds, images, colors, and sometimes even dreams play in your mind, this is the state of hypnagogia where you are being led (the Greek word is "agogos") into the state of sleep (the Greek word is "*hypnos*").

You can utilize this state to aid creativity. Your consciousness is unbound from your body and allowed to flow without your mind thinking of other things. Look for your best and most creative ideas when in this state.

5. Very Deep Trance

Have you slept and not dreamed? This is the deepest level of trance, a place where you can delve into the spiritual and psychological, a place where you can fully explore yourself.

So, how does getting into a trance help in spiritual work? The answer to this question is easily understandable and quite intriguing. When you are awake and functioning, your mind is focused on your body and what is going on around it – there is no limit to the stimulus your body is dealing with. When you enter a trance, you can let go of the physical and allow your mind to think and be.

Trances delve into the subconscious, and we need to remove the conscious, over-thinking mind to get there. It is in the unconscious that our deep-rooted issues and problems live. The conscious or the rational mind is the seat of our ego, whose natural tendency is to keep us safe from perceived and potential dangers, pains, etc.

However, when the ego gets excessively defensive and stubborn about its role, it interferes with our deeper spiritual desires. The overworking ego prevents us from getting rid of old, limiting, and toxic habits and behaviors. It prevents us from releasing and letting go of accumulated and pent-up pain. It comes in the way of our desire to adopt new, healthy habits.

The ego is always on guard, preventing us from waking up sleeping giants buried deep in our minds. Our ego views these sleeping giants as monsters and pain-bearing enemies, and so it creates defense mechanisms to ward off them and keep us "safe." For example, defense mechanisms such as denial, soul-splitting, repressions of trauma, and projections are all defense mechanisms created by our critical mind.

Unfortunately, these defense mechanisms, which the ego considers "safe," offer only superficial comfort and, in reality, are dangerous because they prevent us from connecting with our soul. Consequently, we unwittingly end up with compromised personalities in such a way that our ability to function normally is impacted significantly.

Although supposedly working for our welfare, the ego does not understand that repressing issues and hiding them does not make them disappear. They just remain hidden from view but continue to simmer and grow in strength underneath the mask. These fears and repressed issues grow into monstrous plants and trees within our fertile subconscious minds until they can burst open to create chaos in our world. Sometimes, they don't burst open but continue to nag us until we find the strength to break ego barriers and face them.

Entering a state of trance kills the ego allowing us to bypass its created barriers and connect directly with the unconscious mind and all the hidden, repressed monsters, thereby facilitating healing.

Spiritually, trance states allow Shamans to cross the barrier of their subconscious minds and delve deeper into other realms. They can connect with spiritual guide animals, commune with ancestors and even touch their own soul, the element that's connected to the ultimate divine. Trance states give us a pathway to what is beyond our reality.

Regardless of the theories and beliefs, there is no doubt that trance states help Shamans (and us, if we wish) to access our subconscious mind and from there to the bigger web of the Collective Unconscious space where otherworldly beings live.

Achieving the Shamanic State of Consciousness

Human consciousness can be altered in numerous ways, including through breathwork, meditations, self-hypnosis, visualizations, drugs, and more. A range of mind-body practices can help one achieve an altered or Shamanic state of consciousness.

Shamanic Trance through Breathwork

Breathwork involves altering the pace and rhythm of your breath. It is one of the most commonly used methods to achieve Shamanic trance. Pranayama, one of the oldest and most treasures breathwork practices, is a great way to start using this method. Pranayama calms your body, which, in turn, calms your mind. When we are in a state of calm, our everyday problems don't cloud our judgment or take our focus.

Holotropic Breathwork was developed by Christina and Stanislav Grof. The breathing in this method is quick and rhythmic and is also beneficial when achieving a trance-like state.

The word holotropic comes from two Greek words, "*holos*" meaning whole, and "*trepein*," meaning "to turn, or change." Therefore, holotropic translates to "moving forward wholeness."

This breathing technique brings about healing from within you as you practice it.

The basic principle behind the creation of this breathwork is that every human being is endowed with an inner radar that helps us determine the most important experience we are having at any given point in time. However, we cannot know the experience beforehand and end up realizing it only after it happens. Practitioners try to figure out these experiences as they practice the holotropic breathwork.

This breathwork is done under the strict supervision of a trained and qualified mentor or facilitator and is practiced in a group setting, although individuals can do it on their own after learning and mastering the technique. In a group setting, people are paired off so that one is the "breather" and the other is the "sitter."

The sitter only helps support the breather, which is the active participant in the breathwork. The sitter ensures the breather remains safe right through the session as the breather lies down on a mat and has to breathe with eyes closed. The facilitator guides the session by giving instructions on when and how to alter the rhythm and pace of breathing.

As the pace of breathing increases, care is taken that the breathing is even and no complications arise. The session normally lasts 2-3 hours, during which time repetitive music is played which promotes the breather's desire to achieve a Shamanic state of consciousness. The music is aligned with the speed of breathing. It starts with the drumming sound, reaches a crescendo, and slowly starts tapering off until soft, low meditative music is played.

When the session is up, the participants discuss their experiences, and then the sitter and breather exchange roles. The whole process is repeated for the former sitter and the current breather.

Holotropic breathwork can be unsettling and overwhelming for people, at least in the initial days of practice. It is best to learn it through guided workshops conducted by trained and qualified facilitators before attempting it on your own. Yet, as long as there is no fear of hyperventilating or any other serious lung issue, it is alright to push yourself as it can lead to a Shamanic trance. It is also not advised for people with serious psychological issues. It is vital that you learn from a trained facilitator, ensuring you have no issues before trying it on your own.

The simplest form of breathwork is to breathe in and out slowly and deeply. Use mindful breathing techniques to focus on your breath to enhance the experience of simple but effective breathwork. With persistent practice, your trance state can go from being very light to achieving deeper levels.

Shamanic Trance through Prayer and Mantra

Mantras are prayers, phrases, or sounds that are repeated over and over again to achieve the altered state of consciousness. Many monks and priests belonging to various religions across the globe use prayer and mantra chanting to achieve Shamanic trance.

Shamanic Trance by Staring

This method is simple but effective. Find a comfortable sitting position, preferably somewhere quiet. Find a point or an object at eye level and stare at it. Focus on that point alone and try to concentrate on it while also being aware of all that's around you. You can practice this for a couple of minutes each day. With repeated practice, you'll soon be able to touch various levels of trance states.

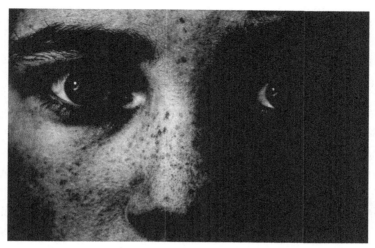

Shamanic Trance through Primal Rhythms and Beats

Shamans commonly use drumming, primal rhythms, and repetitive beats to achieve an altered state of consciousness. You can make your own drum or rattle, or buy one and keep drumming as you sit and listen to the repetitive sounds. Alternatively, you can download drumming recordings and play them in the background while you sit still and meditate or stare at a point or object.

While music is fine when trying to gain a trance, avoid spoken word where you can. Our minds are attuned to language, and you can lose focus when there is conversation around you.

Shamanic Trance through Physical and Emotional Catharsis

As with any activity, if you are tired, you are not going to be in the best state to attain a trance. There is also a danger that you could fall asleep instead of finding the trance state. Indigenous tribes use vigorous dancing to become physically exhausted so that the conscious, rational mind goes into rest mode, leaving the path free to connect with the unconscious mind.

Emotional catharsis happens through long periods of isolation. When left with your own thoughts for days on end, you can achieve a trance-like state of consciousness. This is the reason why people go out on solo trips to feel refreshed and rejuvenated. In ancient times, novices were required to spend months in isolation in the wilderness before they were initiated into the Shamanic tradition. Emotional and physical catharsis was a key element in achieving trance states.

Shamanic Trance through Self-Hypnosis

Self-hypnosis is a powerful tool with the potential for impactful psycho-spiritual transformation. There is a misconception about hypnosis that it is something used wrongly to "control" others' minds (perhaps rooted in stage performances or the fear of being "controlled" by others). Authentic hypnosis is very safe. Further, you are always in control of yourself because no one can really control your mind unless you give your permission at some level. You can follow these simple steps for self-hypnosis:

- Lie down in a dark, quiet room.
- Focus on your breath.
- Repeat *deep sleep, sleep, deep sleep...*

Within a few moments of repeating this, you'll feel a sense of warmth and calmness envelop your body and mind. Your body and mind become completely relaxed. The more you keep trying it, the better you'll become at achieving trance states.

Shamanic Trance through Visualization

Visualization is an easy method that most people use to achieve trance states. If your imagination is good, then this method can work really well for you. You can use a pre-recorded audio for the visualization or download one from the Internet to use. Here are some simple steps to help you with visualization:

- Sit in a quiet, undisturbed place
- Feel your body becoming light and airy
- Visualize your body lifting off the ground
- Imagine yourself soaring like a bird

Use any powerful visualization that suits you best to achieve varying degrees of trance states. Additionally, you can use essential oils and incense to complement the primary method used. For example, if you are doing breathwork or practicing mindfulness meditation, you can burn incense or apply essential oil to your body to enhance your efforts to achieve heightened awareness.

How to Use Trance States

Once you are in a state of trance, regardless of the level you achieve, you can attempt many things. Here are some ideas for you.

- Repeat empowering and loving affirmations – this is a powerful way to change negative, limiting beliefs.

- Request your animal allies and spirit guides to communicate.

- Communicate with divine beings and spirits.

- Connect with your inner child for healing purposes.

- Recall a forgotten memory or dream.

- Access altered states of consciousness.

And as you already know, Shamans undertake Shamanic journeys during trance states.

And finally, another powerful way for Shamans to get into Shamanic trances is discussed in detail in Chapter 15, entitled "Magical Plants to Enhance Sight." Do check that chapter for more information on how plants can boost this step.

Chapter 8: Journeying through the Lower World

The spirit worlds that Shamans visit during their trance states belong to three different categories, including:

- The Lower World

- The Middle World

- The Upper World

Some traditions of Shamanism further divide these three worlds into subworlds. But the primary worlds are the ones mentioned above, and they are the territory of Shamanic journeys all over the world. These are not physical places but are potent energetic domains. While in their trance state, a Shaman travels to one of these worlds, most often accompanied by a power, a spirit guide, or helper.

As you already know, there are various ways Shamans achieve a Shamanic trance. Also, Shamans often use the Axis Mundi or the World Tree to make these journeys. The Axis Mundi connects the three worlds. Shamans travel along the trunk of the tree to the middle, upper, and lower worlds.

Every world has its own vibrations and atmosphere, and these elements were briefly discussed in Part One of this book. Shamans choose the world to visit according to their needs. They learn to make the right choice from years of journeying experience. Also, different intentions call for visits to different worlds.

For example, for advice on a new project or job, a specific spirit or guide from the Upper world could help you make progress. For healing purposes, Shamans normally visit the Lower World, but sometimes, healing <u>may</u> also call for a visit to the Upper World. Experience teaches Shamans the right path to take. More than one journey may be undertaken to achieve the same task.

This chapter is dedicated to a detailed study of the Lower World, the realm of the soul, and the place where all the records of human history are stored.

Understanding the Lower World

Shamans use the help of the Axis Mundi to reach the Lower World, deep inside the earth. They find an opening like a tunnel or a rabbit hole to descend downward. The opening could be a narrow slit at the base of the Axis Mundi, an animal hole on the ground, a staircase going downward, or a cave opening at the base of or behind a waterfall.

The Lower World is deeply associated with transformation and power. It is the place where you can travel to heal and recover lost pieces of your soul. These pieces lost in the labyrinth of time do not go away. They remain in the Lower World, hoping to be rejoined at their original place.

The spirit helpers here usually take the shape of animals and are referred to as power animals or totem animals. But spirit helpers also come in other forms in the Lower World. Sometimes, they whisper advice to you like the wind. Sometimes, trees and plants talk to you. These are nothing but spirit helpers in disguise. Even ancestor spirits can be encountered in the Lower World. There is no strict format or form that spirit helpers take to help us.

Your relationship with the spirit helpers of the Lower World forms the foundation of your Shamanic practice. These guides not only take you around the Lower World but also become excellent lifelong counselors in your path to becoming a good, compassionate Shaman.

Nearly all Shamans keep visiting the Lower World not only to traipse through the endless, wondrous landscapes there but also for healing and transformational work and for their personal growth and learning in the world of Shamanism.

Preparing to Journey to the Lower World

Journeying to the Lower World is rife with danger because it is filled with conflicting emotions and turmoil. It is imperative that you prepare yourself well before undertaking this journey if you unwittingly bring dangerous elements back into your real world. What has to be left there should not be touched.

When you journey to the Lower World, you'll visualize your subtle energy body descending into it. You'll first meet the gatekeeper, the archetypal spirit guarding the gateway to the unconscious mind. The gatekeeper is known by several names. Among the Incas, he is known as "Huascar," which translates to "the one who brings us together." He is portrayed symbolically as a vine or a rope linking the Middle and Lower Worlds.

Before entering the Lower World, you must get this gatekeeper's permission to enter. Usually, he also gives guidance if you handle him with respect and maturity. He will escort you to your destination or power animal and offer counsel about the journey. You should not enter the Lower World without his permission because you are likely to get stuck there if you do. As the gatekeeper, he holds the authority to allow people to enter and exit.

The first journey is normally about finding your spirit, power, and totem animals. Also, the first journey is about connecting with Mother Earth, considering you'll be diving deep into her heart. Mother Earth represents all things feminine. She is the Great Mother who has solutions for all our problems. Deepening your connection with her will empower you significantly.

Before you travel down to the Lower World, you must learn to open sacred space for your journey and close it after returning safely. Sacred space can be created anywhere and at any time. It can be somewhere in the wild, or it can be in a quiet, undisturbed part of your home. The undisturbed aspect is critical as journeys can take time, and you do not want interruptions that not only disturb your session but can also cause harm as your interactions with spiritual beings could get abruptly cut off.

Use these invocations to open sacred space (after you have chosen your sacred space and performed smudging for protection) for your journeying ritual.

Turn to the south and say, *"I call upon the winds of the south to wrap their protectiveness around this sacred space. I call upon the Great Serpent to teach us how to shed our past just as it sheds its old skin for new. Teach us how to walk on the earth softly and without hurting anyone."*

Turn to the west and say, *"I call upon the winds of the west to shower their protective energy on us. May the Jaguar protect our medicines and teach us how to live in peace and in harmonious communion with the universe."*

Turn to the north and say, *"I call upon the winds of the north, and the wisdom of the elderly and the experienced to keep us safe and send us messages through the winds. Oh, ancient ones, we invite you to come hither and warm yourselves at our fire. We honor you who have come before us and those that come after us."*

Turn to the east and say, *"I call upon the winds of the east, bring the power of the rising sun to our space. Oh great eagle, keep us safe under your wings and teach us to fly high."*

Look down and say, *"Mother Earth, we come to you seeking healing medicines on behalf of all those who have walked before us, walk with us, and will walk after us on your blessed land. Keep us safe and protected."*

Look up at the sky and say, *"Father Sky, protect us with your vastness. Keep this space as safe as you hold the stars, the sun, and the moon."*

You can now start your Shamanic journey to the Lower World. After you have finished your journey and returned to your physical world, remember to close the sacred space. Follow the same procedure for closing it and add a line of gratitude with every prayer or supplication. Release their energies back into the cosmos when you are done.

The Journey to the Lower World

When your sacred space is ready, sit within its protected confines. Make yourself comfortable and rest your hands on your knees. Close your eyes and repeat the following breathing rhythm:

- Breathe in for a count of seven.

- Hold for a count of seven

- Breathe out for a count of seven

- Hold for a count of seven.

Repeat this as long as you can. Remember, this exercise is deceptively easy for first-timers, and you may feel giddy-headed. This feeling is the doorway to an altered state of consciousness. Keep practicing the opening of the sacred space ritual and the breathing exercise mentioned above until you can easily enter and exit out of the Shamanic state. A journey to the Lower World helps novice Shamans find their spirit, power, and totem animals.

Understanding Spirit, Power, and Totem Animals

So, what are spirit, power, and totem animals? Let's look at each of them in a bit of detail.

Discovering Your Spirit Animal

Spirit animals form an integral part of all forms of Shamanism practiced across the globe. They act as spiritual guides who manifest themselves in ways we are willing to see them. Often, you feel connected to a particular animal, and spirit guides take the form of these animals to help you in your journey as a Shaman. If you are unsure of which animal you feel connected to, here are some tips to help you get started:

> • Find out about the animal connections in your family and lineage. Regardless of where you live today, discover your roots, and find out which animals represent your original culture because they hold a lot of power for your psyche, considering the energy of these animals has been passed down for generations in your lineage.

> • In fact, some Native Americans request non-Native Americans not to replicate or use the symbols of their spirit animals because there is a distinct connection to the Natives that non-Natives cannot feel or connect with.

> • Pay attention to your dreams. Do you see a particular animal appearing in your dreams repeatedly? Make entries in your dream journal (more about dream journals later in this book).

> • What were your favorite animals in your childhood? Did you have a beloved pet? Did you come across wild animals as a child?

Find answers to these questions, and soon you are likely to find your spirit animal, the animal that your spirit guide takes the form of to help and guide you through your various Shamanic journeys. You can use the journeying ritual described under "Discovering Your Power Animal" to go into the Lower World and find your spirit animal.

Discovering Your Power Animal

Power animals are also found in the Lower World, and they, like spirit animals, will guide you in your Shamanic journey. The difference is that the power animal you find in the Lower World will accompany you back to your real world. Your power animal can be anything from a simple, common swallow to a gigantic, seemingly frightening crocodile. Insects are avoided because they are closely associated with the Lower World, and it is best to leave them there and not bring them back.

So, what is the role of your power animal? It does not represent who you are becoming, nor does it symbolize your dreams and desires. It represents your natural, unspoiled state. You may even retrieve a powerful animal that you dislike. For example, you could pick a scorpion, snake, or any other animal you are frightened of or find revolting. Even then, this becomes your power animal because it represents an instinctual part of yourself that you disconnected for the same reasons that you dislike or find tasteful in your animal.

Your power animal will ground you and keep you connected to your authentic, instinctual self. You can learn lessons from it by communicating with it, by learning and mimicking its movements, the way it lives, its rhythms, etc. Follow these steps to journey to the Lower World to find your power animal.

Record these instructions in your own voice so that you can use them for your journey

Sit comfortably in a quiet, undisturbed place. You can fix your gaze on an object just above your line of vision, or you can close your eyes. Join your hands near your heart in a prayer pose. Repeat this intention, "*I want to get in touch with my power animal and retrieve it from the Lower World.*"

Next, open the sacred space using the ritual mentioned in this chapter and do the breathing exercise while following the instructions. When you are ready, you can start your journey to the Lower World to find your power animal.

Find the opening at the root of the Axis Mundi and look down it. See the long-winding staircase descending down into the Earth.

Step onto this staircase and keep moving downwards until you find the doorway opening into the Lower World. Knock on the door and wait for the doorkeeper to open it.

When he does, ask his permission to enter. Step across the doorway when he gives his permission.

Walk down the narrow path flanked by dense bushes. Keep walking until you reach a vast, green meadow that stretches into the horizon. Find a stone in this meadow and sit on it.

Wait for the power animal to approach you. Breathe calmly as you wait, and sense the animal approaching from behind.

Sense the animal's eyes resting on you. Feel the hair on your neck stand up as it comes closer to you.

Hear the rhythm of its breathing as it comes very close to you.

When you feel that your power animal is ready to receive you, gently stand up and turn around. Look into the eyes of your power animal.

- Reach out to touch its fur, fins, beak, antlers, scales, or the relevant body part.

- Gaze gently into its eyes and ask your questions:
  o What have you brought for me?
  o What heals you? What are the medicines you use?
  o What are your weaknesses?
  o What are your strengths?
  o How long have you known me?
  o How can I take care of you? What food do you eat?

o Why are you my power animal rather than another one?

Engage in a long, deep conversation with your power animal for as long as both of you want. When both of you are ready, invite your power animal to come with you back to your world. Walk back to the doorway and get permission from the gatekeeper to leave with your power animal. Find the staircase and walk up, ensuring your power animal follows you.

When you reach the opening at the root of the Axis Mundi, help your power animal come up and allow it to roam your world freely. Reach out and touch your animal and feel its energy merge with your own. Move your body in the same way as your power animal moves. Try to match your rhythm with its rhythm. Learn to speak its language. Teach your language to it. When you feel satisfied with your first interaction with your power animal, ask its permission to return to your world and let it know that the two of you'll always be together.

Slowly open your eyes and become aware of your physical surroundings. Feel the physical sensations and slowly bring about awareness in your physical body. Feel your energy now merged with the energy of your power animal. When your ritual is finished, give thanks and close the sacred space. Now, your power animal is part of you, and you can interact with it in any way you want. Connect with it and seek the part of your soul it represents. Remember, your power animal usually represents that part of yourself that you don't like or are trying to forget.

For a while, engage with your power animal in the real world. When you get up every morning, stretch the way your power animal would. When you shake hands with people, do it by incorporating the spirit of your power animal and its actions. Cohabitate with your power animal until you become it.

Embodying your power animal empowers you to become increasingly reliant on your instinctive powers. You'll find it easy to connect with your intuitive power and use it to guide your rational mind to live the life you desire. Most importantly, your power animal will protect that part of you that you hated and that has now come home to you again.

Discovering Totem Animals

The concept of totem animals is based on the Native American belief that each of us is associated with nine different animals whose power and energy complement our energy right through our life. Different totem animals emerge and retract depending on our needs and our direction in our lives. A totem serves as the emblem of a tribe, family, clan, and individuals. Members of the clan are not allowed to kill their totem animals.

Totem animals remain with you for your entire life, keeping you company in the physical and spiritual worlds. While power animals and spirit animals will be there as well, in some native cultures, it is believed that your totem animals become your lifelong, primary spiritual guardians.

Choosing your totem animal calls for looking out for the right signs and interpreting them correctly. The practice of discovering your totem animal is a highly spiritual and therapeutic experience. You could find your totem animal in a moment of spiritual or religious epiphany. Alternatively, you could find it through a simple, practical lesson of wisdom in the real world. You can use the journeying ritual described under "Discovering Your Power Animal" to go into the Lower World and find your totem animal.

Here is a small list of animals commonly used in Shamanism as power, spirit, and totem animals and their core qualities:

- **Ant** – These tiny creatures represent teamwork and the never-give-up spirit.

- **Alligator** – This powerful creature is known for its stealth and its resilience to survive in any difficult situation.

- **Armadillo** – Represents and appreciates the importance of personal boundaries. It always carries protection.

- **Antelope** – This swift animal represents quick and efficient action.

- **Butterfly** – These beautiful insects represent the power of transformation and growth. Known for its resilience, it is incredibly adaptable and represents ease and grace.

- **Badger** – The badger stands for drive, passion, and aggressiveness, reminding you that these qualities are critical to living a life of meaning and purpose.

- **Bear** – Bear bears a deep connection to the earth and the outdoors. A bear is deeply emotional.

- **Cat** – Symbolizing independence, curiosity, and adventure, a cat, is the master of patience.

- **Dove** – A dove is a symbol of peace and represents new beginnings, and is also known for optimism and hopefulness.

- **Dolphin** – Symbolizing playfulness combined with wisdom; dolphins are Masters of Communication.

- **Deer** – Deer are highly intuitive and sensitive, striking a graceful balance between success, confidence, and gentleness.

- **Elephant** – Also representing wisdom, elephants manifest spiritual understanding and gentleness despite their size and strength.

- **Fox** – A master at the art of camouflage, a fox is a master of detachment too. Yet, a fox is at peace with its surroundings.

- **Frog** – Frogs help in physical and emotional healing. This animal is a reminder that we have to check with our past, heal from its wounds and move on.

- **Hawk** – This bird stands for all-around perceptiveness. It is also a highly compassionate and empathetic bird.

- **Horse** – A horse stands for passion, drive, and productivity.

- **Lion** – The lion is a symbol of courage. A natural-born leader is a sign of authority.

- **Mouse** – The mouse represents the importance of scrutiny and detail. It reminds us not to overlook the small things in our lives.

- **Owls** – With the power to see what many others miss; owls know the deeper meaning of things. They have the power to discover life's hidden treasures.

- **Peacock** – This gorgeous animal represents reinvention and resurrection. It reminds us that it is never too late for positive transformation.

- **Tiger** – This striped, wondrous animal stands for raw emotions. It is endowed with outstanding instinctive powers.

- **Turtle** – This animal is highly spiritual, and its long life is a representation of the long but fruitful journey towards truth and wisdom.

- **Wolf** – The wolf is also connected with intuitive powers. It represents freedom and intelligence. It puts primal instincts over everything else.

Some Personal Stories

When Nancy began walking the Shamanic path, she was riddled with doubts about her spirit guides. She lived in the heart of New York, a concrete jungle where seeing or meeting with animals except pets (and usually cats and dogs). She wondered how she would find her power animal.

Her mentor and guide, Susan, told her to relax and said that Mother Nature would find a way to send her signs that led to her power animal. Just trust her and wait, keeping your heart, mind, and body open to receiving messages from beyond.

Nancy diligently practiced journeying to the Lower World in various ways. Her favorite means to achieve the Shamanic trance were rhythmic, repetitive drumbeats. She would lock herself in her room every Saturday, ensuring she was undisturbed until nighttime. She would journey down to the Lower World every Saturday afternoon.

The first time she journeyed down, she thought she got a glimpse of a strange sight. For an almost imperceptible instant, she saw a hawk riding on the back of a wolf – headed her way. She sensed them for an instant. She turned immediately, perhaps too soon, because she saw nothing after that.

She went back many times down to the Lower World but to no avail. She had journeyed so many times that the gatekeeper would wave her in, giving her a smile. He reassured her about finding her desire when she sought advice from him regarding the discovery of her power animal. Once, he had said, "Don't worry. Persist in your search. If there is a delay, then it could mean you'll be rewarded doubly for your relentless persistence." She couldn't understand but never gave up her efforts.

And finally, one day, she got her answer. While walking on the streets of her neighborhood, she saw an underground pub, and its sign read, "The Hawk and the Wolf." The brand icon of the cafe was startlingly similar to the fleeting vision she had on her first journey to the Lower World. It was as if some spark was lit, and she glowed with power and wisdom in the exploding light.

Nancy quickly went back home and prepared to journey again to the Lower World. This time, she took her time waiting at the same stone that she sat on when she saw the hawk and wolf vision for the first time. She stayed there unmoving, waiting! After a long time, she sensed the sounds of the wolf's feet on the ground.

She was dying to look back but stayed put, fearing the animals might think she was being excessively hasty. Very soon, she sensed the breath of the wolf close to her. She heard the flutter of wings. Slowly, she turned and found the same vision, that of the gray wolf with the hawk sitting firmly on its back. She looked at their eyes, and they stared unblinkingly. She knew she had found her totem and power animals.

She spoke at length with both of them. She realized that they were checking her persistence and diligence in meeting them. They had appeared to her as soon as they were convinced she was ready to take a big step into the world of Shamanism.

Only when she returned from her journey did she feel the drive to find out more about her roots. She was an orphan and was brought up in an orphanage in New York. She went back there and got her mother's details. From there, she had a fascinating personal journey.

Nancy found out that her mother had Native American roots. She was able to get in touch with a close friend of her mother's, who took her to meet another contact. She kept doing this until she found out that she was part of the culturally rich Bird and Wolf Clans of the Cherokee tribe.

She then realized that Shamanism was in her genes, and in some deep part of her inner self, she knew she was meant to take the path of her ancestors. Nancy studied advanced Shamanism from a wise member of the Cherokee tribe and went on to build strong, robust Shamanic roots for herself.

Like Nancy, once your calling to become a Shaman is clear, then Mother Nature will find a way to lead you to your rightful place with the help of your spirit, power, and totem animals. So, go on and try the techniques mentioned in this chapter and begin the exciting journeys to the Lower World.

Chapter 9: Exploring the Middle World, Our Home

This chapter deals with the Middle World, which represents the reality we live in. The Middle World consists of our real, earthly world and all the related spiritual dimensions and soul aspects. The Middle World includes everything in the real world but without the veils of ignorance covering them. So, Shamans journeying to the Middle World can connect with spirits and soul aspects of nature beings, the past elements of the earth, and the future elements.

Shamans journey to the Middle World to find out specific information regarding an event or place on earth. Usually, this kind of journeying happens when the Shaman needs to work with the soul of a specific place or some aspect of nature. Often, for rituals, Shamans need to collaborate with the forces and spirits of the Middle World.

As the Middle World is a reflection of our real world, a Shamanic journey through this world is best achieved through astral projection. But before we move on to astral projection and how to do it, let us try and explain the Middle World in a bit more detail.

Understanding the Middle World

As you already know, the Middle World consists of your physical reality, along with the beings and spirits that you cannot normally see or talk to in the physical world. The Middle World is a reflection of our world along with all its hidden layers. It is the spiritual dimension of the physical world where you can see and experience the unseen.

Journeying to the Middle World is all about finding your anchor spot. This place refers to the most comfortable place for you to identify and access the Axis Mundi. The anchor spot acts like a safe spot, a place you can retreat to when you feel any kind of danger or difficulty as you delve deeper into more complex journeys into the Three Worlds.

Find a happy place that you like. It could be a park that you frequented as a child. It could be a beautiful beach where you found your first love. It could be a glade where you find calm and peace. It could even be your favorite spot in your home. Just ensure the place is slightly big so that you can see and sense the surroundings with all their elements. The more you engage with your senses, the more powerful your visualizations will be.

Use any method (for novices, repetitive drumming rhythms work really well) to get into a trance state. Alternatively, you can use the methods described in the previous chapter to begin your journey into the Middle World.

Sit in any comfortable position and let the drum beating start. When you get into a trance state, visualize your favorite place. What do you see, smell, touch, feel? Just engage with all the elements in your favorite spot. If it is a small clearing in a forest area, look around and see what kinds of plants and trees are growing in the area.

What sounds do you hear? Can you see any animals around? What do you smell? Do you see other people in the vicinity? Make sure you don't disturb anything because they could also be on their own journeys. Remember, when you are on a Shamanic journey, you'll be in the Collective subconscious region where all the subconscious minds of all spirits and beings are found.

Familiarize yourself with this spot. Find the Axis Mundi in that place. Observe its vast system of roots at the base of the tree. Find an opening or hole that will take you down into the Lower World. You can use this opening for your journeys into the Lower World.

Observe its powerful, gigantic trunk rising upwards toward the limitless sky. Observe its interlocking system of branches and leaves. Observe its wide canopy of leaves at the peak of the tree. See if you can find the ladder that will take you up when you begin your journey to the Upper World. Make a note of this ladder and its position.

The most important aspect of your first journey to the Middle World is to familiarize yourself with this anchor spot. As you make more and more journeys, this place will undergo changes as you add, delete, and/or alter elements in it, incorporating lessons you learned helpful spirits you have met. The totem animal you brought back from the Lower World would most likely find its home here.

Journeying to the Middle World is also done to visit beings associated with Mother Nature. You could visit the Middle World to learn from trees, plants, animals, insects, minerals, etc. Keep your senses open to receive messages from anywhere. You could hear a plant speaking to you, giving you advice on using its parts for healing. You could see a flower beckoning you to give you an important message. The wind may touch you, wanting to share something with you.

A note of warning about the Middle World is that it is the place where spirits of deceased souls who have not yet crossed over are found. These souls usually belong to those people who met with traumatic deaths and have not been able to come to terms with their death. You could even meet spirits who are not aware of their deaths. They believe they are still alive.

As a beginner, you are unlikely to know how to help these spirits. It is best to avoid them politely and go on your way. However, it is perfectly alright to speak to and interact with the spirits of all elements of nature, including the trees, plants, tree and plant parts, rivers, mountains, streams, etc. You could also meet with fairies, devas, elves, and other spirits of supernatural beings in the Middle World.

Astral Projection

What is astral projection? Astral projection, also called out-of-body experience, is one of the most wondrous and beautiful spiritual practices that help you move beyond the limits of the physical world. When done correctly and persistently, astral projection experiences can help you gain clarity and purpose. It is an excellent tool for growth and development in the field of Shamanism.

You can use astral projection to find out your own personal, deeply-embedded, forgotten truths, or you can use it to travel to outer space and back. Regardless of the purpose, this experience is exhilarating, transformative, rejuvenating, and easily doable by all of us. Astral projection is not some performance magic. It is something that happens to all of us naturally.

For example, many of us have dreams of flying to pay a visit to a known or unknown place. The sensations of this flying experience are so real that when you wake up from your dream, you feel lost. You feel disoriented from your physical surroundings. It is as if you have been suddenly thrust back into your body.

There are umpteen stories of yogis and saints, especially from the Eastern part of the world, where they have visited devotees staying far away while their bodies remained in a meditative pose in the place of residence. Similarly, many sick people have been healed by saints and medicine men from remote areas who have performed astral travel for this purpose.

The dreams and the stories are both real and have happened. We are not talking about scammers. We are talking about real, authentic stories that seem marvelous but are actually possible in our world through the concept of astral projection. This concept is based on the belief that we have two bodies, namely the physical body and the astral body.

In dreams, our astral body travels to other planes of consciousness and returns just before it knows you'll wake up. Sometimes, the return happens suddenly, and that's why you feel you have been thrust back into your body. Sometimes, the return will be gradual, and, at these times, you'll get a surreal feeling as if you really traveled to some unknown place. Yes, the feeling is real because your astral body has traveled, and you didn't even realize it.

And the best part is that astral travel, like mindfulness meditation and other spiritual activities, can be practiced, learned, and mastered. You can have out-of-body experiences in your conscious state. You'll see the astral plane is solid and firm and, at the same time, amorphous and changeable. Time in the astral plane feels distorted. In the astral plane, multiple planes of realities and realms exist. All of them can be visited by experienced astral travelers.

In Shamanism, astral projection works brilliantly to travel to the Middle World because it is a reflection of the real world. The astral projection will help you see and experience your own world but with all the hidden realities and realms exposed for your benefit. You'll be able to meet and connect with all the spirits and beings living in the unseen part of the real world. It may be difficult for novices to experience everything. However, the more you practice, the better you'll get.

The first thing to do before you begin your astral projection journey is to learn to conquer fear. You have to remind yourself that your astral body is firmly attached to your physical body and that you can return whenever you want to. The control to go and come is in your hands. Nobody else can control you. Yet, it is important to protect both your astral and physical bodies before you begin the journey. Dangerous and harmful spirits also reside in the astral plane.

Do not try astral projection practices while under the influence of drugs and alcohol. It is very dangerous and can even lead to temporary (and even permanent) insanity on rare occasions. Follow these steps for a safe astral projection experience:

First of all, meditate for a few minutes until you feel completely calm and relaxed.

Next, fill your mind with positive thoughts and feelings. Recall a happy occasion and relive that experience.

Think of your friends and family with positive thoughts. As long as your positivity and spirited nature remain strong and intact, negative forces will not be able to touch you.

Fill your mind with positive thoughts about the upcoming astral projection experience. The reason for this is that astral travelers will actually encounter what they themselves project into the astral plane, so positivity is essential.

Before taking off, visualize a circle of white light keeping you safe and protected. Imagine the white light encircling and enveloping your body for protection.

Visualize a pair of beautiful, elegant hands emerging from this envelope of white light. Imagine those hands cleansing and clearing your aura, ensuring every bit of negativity is removed from the tip of your toes to the top of your head.

You can begin the journey when you feel completely satisfied with your protection measures and feel completely safe.

Let meditational music or drumming beats surround the space. It is better to do this activity while sitting because you can easily fall asleep if you lie down. Then the experience might be the same as dreaming in an unconscious state.

Banish all other thoughts and clear your mind completely. To help you to do this, imagine all your thoughts flowing into a clay pot. When the pot is full, visualize yourself breaking it and releasing all the thoughts into the cosmos.

Focus on your breathing. Breathe in through your nose and breathe out through your mouth.

Visualize yourself sitting peacefully in your anchor spot. Imagine a peaceful, calm scene where all the elements are also calm and relaxed, either going about their work undisturbed or sitting like you and peacefully meditating.

When you are fully relaxed, chant in your mind, "I rise, I float, I fly." Keep doing this, and soon you'll realize that you have entered into a Shamanic state. You'll feel light and airy inside and yet powerfully conscious. Your level of awareness will be acutely heightened. Interestingly, your body will feel heavy and relaxed.

Continue chanting "I rise, I float, I fly," and, as you chant, visualize your astral body rising up from your physical body. Watch it float further and further away from your physical body, with the connecting cord preventing it from flying away from you. You may not reach this stage in the initial days of practice. Sometimes, the astral body climbs up a few feet and jumps back into your physical body.

Disappointment at failing mustn't deter you from regular, diligent practice. It takes persistent, enduring practice to get your astral body to leave your physical body, knowing it is safe and can come back any time.

Astral travel is similar to traveling in a moving vehicle. Keep moving, and soon you'll see a burst of light and color ahead of you. That's the astral plane and the vision of the Middle World. Here, you'll find the reflection of your real-world and other spirits and beings not seen in the real world. Go around and explore the Middle World as much as you want.

If you have come seeking something, go around and try to discover it. Ask your spirit, power, and totem animals to help you. Your totem animal will have already done a lot of exploration on your behalf. You can explore the Middle World with it and accept its help to find what you seek. When you are ready to come back, all you need to do is make the decision to return.

Visualize yourself back in your physical body. Count slowly from 1 to 10, focusing on each body part as you do so, thereby bringing awareness to your entire body. Don't be in any rush. Do it slowly. Next, move each part of your body in turn, starting from the toe and slowly moving upwards until you are fully awake and completely aware of your physical surroundings. Sit quietly in the same position. Rub your hands together to generate heat and apply this heat to your face. Slowly, get up from your sitting position. Remember to make detailed notes of your experiences.

Meditations for Improved Astral Projection Experiences

Astral projection requires out-of-the-box thinking. After all, in such an experience, your soul is going outside your body to roam freely anywhere you want it to. You have to go into a deep meditative state and let go of fear so that you can allow your astral body to leave your physical body to roam around as you wish. Astral projection, when done correctly, will ensure you have control over what happens. So, here are some powerful meditation techniques that will build your astral protection powers.

• Hypnosis

You have already learned that self-hypnosis is a tool used by Shamans to achieve the Shamanic state. Through hypnotherapy, you can also reach this state to do astral traveling. A suggestible hypnotic state raises your consciousness to higher realms.

Hypnosis is nothing but getting into a heightened state of awareness with minimal physical disturbance. This opens up your mind so wide that astral projection experiences can be easily achieved. You can use the following steps to get started with self-hypnosis to aid astral projection.

- Find a quiet, undisturbed place for the practice.

- Set your intention. In this case, you can say loudly (or write it beforehand), "I want to achieve a heightened state of awareness to perform astral traveling." Make sure your purpose is clear.

- Close your eyes and take a couple of deep breaths.

- Start by eliminating all negative thoughts and energies, especially stress and anxiety.

- Focus on your breathing. Make it slow and rhythmic so that all the negative forces and thoughts are chipped away from your mind. Inhale peace and exhale negativity.

- Once you are completely relaxed, imagine your anchor spot, your safe and happy place.

- Affirm your state of peace and calm by repeating the affirmation, "I am happy, safe, and at peace."

  o From here, begin your astral projection experience as described in the previous section.

- **Activation of Chakras**

  o The primary chakras are the seven different energy centers in your body, each representing a different aspect of your being. The seven chakras are:

- Muladhara, or the Root Chakra, is situated at the base of your spine between your genitals and anus. It represents our survival instincts, emotions, and self-sufficiency.

- Svadhisthana, or the Sacral Chakra, is situated in the lower abdomen below the navel and represents our sexuality, creativity, and self-worth.

- Manipura, or the Solar Plexus Chakra, is between the navel and the bottom of the rib cage and represents our ego, aggression, and anger.

- Anahata, or the Heart Chakra, is situated in the heart region and represents love, attachment, trust, compassion, and passion.

- Vishuddha, or the Throat Chakra, is located in the throat area and represents communication, articulation, and expression.

- Ajna, or the Third Eye Chakra, is located in the middle of the forehead between the brows. It represents intuitive knowledge and spirituality.

- Sahasrara, or the Crown Chakra, is located at the top of your head and represents the portal between the physical and the non-physical realms.

- Our innate energy resides at the Muladhara, lying dormant. Through various meditation techniques, you can awaken this dormant energy and lift it through the seven chakras until it reaches the crown chakra, and the doorway to the non-physical realms will open for you. The astral projection will become easy from here.

- **Binaural Beats**

Binaural beats are formed with two separate tones, and when your brain hears these two tones, it tries to enmesh and combine the frequencies, and this brain activity can help you get into the meditative state needed for astral projection. Listening to binaural beats allows different wavelengths of your brain to become synchronized, which boosts your mood and energy levels and helps you achieve a heightened state of awareness.

Try the meditative methods mentioned above to boost your astral projection skills. Slowly but surely, with persistent practice, your ability in astral travel is bound to improve, helping you make journeys to the Middle World for your Shamanic works.

More Tips for Astral Projection

Here are some more tips and suggestions for improved astral projection skills and experience.

Tap Into Your Inherent Capabilities – Remember that astral projection is not something surreal. It happens to all of us in the normal course of life. It is just that many of us are unaware or unconscious when it happens. You do not need to learn anything new here. You simply need to tap into your innate skills to allow your astral body to roam around freely.

Astral projection practice is like working a muscle. The more you make it work, the stronger it gets. Spend a lot of time practicing through visualization and other mind-empowering techniques. Just work on adjusting yourself when you realize that your astral body is separated from your physical body. When you master this element, then astral projection will work easily for you.

Spend Time Meditating and Performing Self-Hypnosis – Meditating is one of the easiest ways to achieve a Shamanic state. Meditating allows you to tap into the deepest aspects of your consciousness. Clear and relax your mind and allow yourself to accept the fact that there is a realm beyond this physical one. You can use self-hypnosis and meditation apps for your practice.

Harness the Power of Crystals – Crystals are commonly used in the world of Shamanism for their myriad energetic powers. While they are excellent tools for healing, they are used for various kinds of help in the astral realm as well. Here is a list of crystals that are very useful in your astral projection practices:

> • **Agate** – Helps you to put your body and mind into a calm, relaxed state.

> • **Rose Quartz** – Helps you to realize that love is more important and useful than fear. Fear is one of the biggest obstacles in astral projection exercises. Most people find it scary that a part of them can leave their bodies and roam freely. This fear creates blockages in their minds preventing them from liberating themselves into this fascinating aspect of spirituality.

> • **Clear Quartz** – Helps to open doors into astral realms

> • **Amethyst** – Helps activate the crown chakra and helps during lucid dreaming (this element will be discussed in the next chapter)

> • **Citrine** – Helps to keep negativity away and makes the journey joyful

> • **Carnelian** – Helps to keep your warrior spirits healthy and strong

- **Aventurine** – Is excellent for emotional stability

- **Hematite** – Strengthens the bond between the spirit and body and helps in grounding too

- **Lapis Lazuli** – Offers wisdom and prophetic magic

- **Tiger's Eye** – For enhancing your spiritual energy and grounding

- **Black Tourmaline** – For protection

Practice in the dark. When you focus on astral projection, the light – which is part of the physical world – tends to distract you from this practice. Moreover, light focuses on elements in your surroundings – which become distractions. You can use sleep masks to ensure your eyes are completely covered and darkness surrounds you.

Don't sit for your practices expecting something spectacular. Let go of your expectations. Simply sit and engage with your practice. When you expect something, it could block or close doorways that are waiting to be opened because your mind is burdened with the expectation. On the contrary, with no expectations, your mind is free to do what it wants, and that's when hidden doorways open, leading you into fascinating astral realms. Walking and exploring the Middle World in this state of mind will bring outcomes way beyond your imagination.

And finally, a word of caution to end this chapter. Astral projection can be a thrilling and exhilarating experience with the power to take your Shamanic skills up a few notches. However, you must take things slowly and allow your body and mind to sync with each other to prevent hazards and dangers. Do not hesitate to ask for the help of a qualified, trained mentor to learn and master the art before you try it on your own.

Chapter 10: Journeying through the Higher World

The Higher World represents the home of guides and spiritual teachers and, therefore, is the most difficult world to access. Yet, many Shamans before having done it, and many more will come who will continue to do these difficult tasks. This chapter is dedicated to the Upper World and how you can access it.

The Upper World is situated very high above this earthly world. It is the place of our spirit and destiny. Shamans travel to increasingly high levels during the trance state to reach the Upper

World. Almost all journeys are undertaken with the help of power animals or a spirit guide that lifts the Shaman up. Shamans "fly" to the Upper World powered by rhythmic drumming and are ably supported by spirit allies.

There is a distinct shift in the vibration in the energetic atmosphere as you move from the Middle World to the Upper World. Sometimes, you know you have reached the Upper World when you float through a thin membrane-like veil that separates it from the lower level.

The powers of the spirit beings of the Upper World are distinctly different from those in the Middle and Lower Worlds. They offer a higher perspective of things and situations, empowering you to distance yourself from difficulties and obstacles. Also, the powers of the spirits in the Upper World can help you discover new, subtle, and finer aspects of yourself.

Methods to Access the Upper World

Two of the most powerful methods to access the Upper World are guided meditation and dreamwork.

Guided Meditations

- Close your eyes and visualize a beautiful beach with blue waters stretching into the horizon.

- You are alone on the beach of white, soft sand

- You sit on it under the shade of a huge boulder and stare into the horizon

- The waves gently touch your feet. You feel their warmth

- A large wave comes gently to you and forms a cup for you to get into

- You climb the water steps formed on the gigantic wave and get into the cup. The interior is spacious, and the floor is lined with soft carpets.

- The wave slowly lifts you up keeps rising upward into the sky

- You feel secure and safe and happy to ride the wave

- It crosses the clouds and comes to a stop at a doorway

- You get out of the cup and knock on the door, which the doorkeeper opens

- With his permission, you enter the Upper World

Working with Dreams

Human beings have been trying to interpret dreams since prehistoric times. Shamans of ancient tribes all across the world took dreams very seriously. Some believed that dreams were messages from the Spirit of the cosmos, while others believed that they were messages from our souls. Ancient Shamans worked with and tried to interpret their own dreams and those of other members of the clan who reported them.

Shamanism is one of the most natural paths leading to spiritual enlightenment. Shamans and other believers honor the Earth and all forms of animate and inanimate objects connected with her. Shamanism acknowledges and reveres the mystery and magic of this cosmos and believes that everything around and within us is endowed with spirit. Shamanism honors the human soul, knowing it is a part of the primary cosmic Spirit. Shamanism defines an enlightened person as one who identifies and recognizes the truth and tries to understand every situation or encounter to reveal its truth.

Shamans believe that waking reality is the same as our dreams when we sleep. It is not that our waking life is false or unreal. It is just that our perception of the wholesomeness of the world is flawed and incomplete. Our mind is capable of just scratching the surface of reality as we see and experience it. This approach results in flawed perceptions, which, in turn, obscures the truth of bigger and greater realities.

When we curtail the powers of our dreams and their potential, we are pushing our unconscious minds into deeper depths than they are already in. Consequently, we are enhancing the difficulty of accessing the energies and powers of our unconscious minds. Shamans believe that a truly enlightened person is one who is awake even when they are asleep. An unenlightened person is one who is asleep even when they are awake.

When we expand our consciousness, break the limitations of the physical world, and accept the idea that there is a plethora of realities that exist in this cosmos, we are building personal strength, but we are also looking at the welfare of the entire human race. A whole body of knowledge and potential beyond our conscious mind is there to help us. And this is the core belief of Shamanism, to access powers seemingly beyond the reach of the physical world and share the benefits with the world.

Dreamwork is about discovering the energetic spirit behind our dreams for the resolution of existing problems. Shamans use dreams as doorways to travel to the Collective Unconscious so that they can get direct access to the unconscious impulse that gave rise to the dream.

The same holds true for nightmares too. The energies in the nightmares, which are sourced in the unconscious mind, can be accessed and then released to free the person from their negative impacts. In the same way, creative energies can be identified and discovered through dreams and released into the physical world to make positive, creative changes in the dreamer's real life.

When you transform, release, or access the energies of the unconscious mind (or your inner self), your conscious mind and physical body (the outer self) also get transformed, leading to a new, happier reality than before. Dreams are seen from multiple perspectives in Shamanism which, in turn, allows us to work with them in various ways depending on the need at a particular point in time. Shamans believe that dreaming could be:

- Undertaking a Shamanic journey

- Having a vision

- Receiving important, relevant information from spirit guides, etc., while in a trance state

From a non-Shamanic perspective, dreams are visions or experiences you have when you sleep. In Shamanism, it is possible to interact with the spirits in your dreams. Shamans see dreams as another reality where the interdependent, interlinked cosmic system rooted in Spirit is expressed and experienced.

The reality in dreams is far more fluid and dynamic than the physical reality. While the non-conventional perspective makes the physical world "real" and the dream world "unreal," Shamans see both as aspects of the same cosmic reality. In fact, since dream-like and dream states are more fluid and dynamic than the real world, it can be said that it is easier to connect with the Spirit in dream states rather than through the rational, conscious mind.

In Shamanism, dreams could represent anything. It could be a visit paid by your spirit guide, power animal, or guardians in a nightly encounter to give you a message. They could come to give you advice or counsel. Sometimes, they could visit you in your dreams for teaching and initiation purposes.

In fact, many Shamans have received their calling through dreams. Michael Harner (1929-2018) was a leading Shaman in the modern world. Backed by years of experience as an anthropologist, Michael Harner founded the Center of Shamanic Studies in 1983. He created a list of ten core principles of dreams. You can use them to understand and interpret your dreams. The ten core principles, according to Michael Harner, are:

1. Spirits are real, and they are an integral part of our world. You have to acknowledge and understand this concept that spirits are everywhere and in varying capacities to correctly understand and interpret your dreams.

2. Spirits form and create all dreams. These spirits could be your own or those of others you have entangled or interacted with.

3. Spirits work in different ways and have different capabilities and preoccupations. The spirits that come in your dream could also be giving you different messages impacting different aspects of your life. Spirits use signs and symbols to communicate with you.

4. Dream-producing spirits could be helping souls or suffering souls. Those helping your soul could be your guardians or spirit helpers.

5. Suffering souls usually come not to help you but to seek help from you. Dreams containing suffering souls (those who have not been able to cross over yet because they have not come to terms with their deaths) are usually nightmares, and you could wake up feeling scared.

6. Nightmares could be dreams produced by suffering spirits, or they could be helpful warnings. A helpful spirit could also use dreams to warn you of underlying health issues you have been ignoring or those that are not yet visibly symptomatic.

7. People with robust spirits are more resistant to dreams of suffering souls than people with low-powered spirits. If you work with your mental and spiritual strength, you'll reduce the risk of getting entangled with suffering souls. The

power of your spirit will serve as a protective shield keeping you safe from unwanted and harmful spirits.

8. Guardian spirits appear in big dreams, those that either happen repeatedly or have such a powerful impact that you have a waking dream. When these guardian spirits appear in your dreams, then they bring clear, purposeful life-guiding messages that can transform your life and even change the course of your life.

9. These principles are applicable to all types of dreams, including waking, sleeping, visions, and daydreams. These Shamanic principles can be applied to any sort of spontaneous dream that you have no control over.

10. You can use the guidance of a Shamanic practitioner or guide or by merging your spirit with that of your spiritual guide to relook at the dream and discover its hidden messages in signs and symbols. You can reimagine your non-voluntary dream and pick up crucial insights.

Interpreting your dreams is not an easy task. You first have to learn to master the skill of understanding metaphors from a spiritual perspective. Use the following Dream Yoga exercise to increase your ability to recall your dreams. When you have mastered this exercise, you can move on to lucid dreaming.

Dream Yoga

Keep a pen and notebook by the side of your bed before falling asleep. Take a glass of water and drink half of it. Then, tell yourself loudly, "When I wake up, I will drink the other half, and then recall my dream." Set your clock to wake you up a few minutes before your actual normal wake-up time. Preferably, use soft music instead of blaring alarms or the sound of some talk show.

If you are likely to wake up during the night to visit the bathroom, then keep a recorder close by so that you can record any dream (interrupted or completed) you got just before you woke up. Immediately on getting up in the morning, drink the remaining water and lie back on your bed.

Close your eyes, allowing the images of your dreams to play back into your awareness. Open your eyes and record what you saw in your dream journal (more on dream journals later on in this chapter). Keep practicing this on a daily basis, and soon your ability to recall your dreams will improve significantly.

What Is Lucid Dreaming?

In a research paper entitled <u>Volitional Components of Consciousness Vary Across Wakefulness, Dreaming and Lucid Dreaming</u>, published in January 2014 in the NIH journal by Martin Dresler and team, lucid dreaming was described as follows,

> *"In contrast to the restricted consciousness of normal dreaming, the rare state of lucid dreaming is characterized by full-blown consciousness including all higher-order aspects: the sleeping subject is no longer deluded by the dream narrative but becomes fully aware of the true nature of his current state of consciousness. This wake-like intellectual clarity comprises restored access to memory functions, including increased availability of self-related information and fully realized agency, enabling the dreamer to volitionally execute his intentions within the dream narrative. Lucid dreaming can be trained, which makes this phenomenon a promising research topic despite its rarity in untrained subjects."*

In common language, lucid dreaming is a dream in which you are aware that you are dreaming and therefore have the power to control how the dream happens. Awareness of dream states played a big role in Eastern religious philosophies such as Buddhism. Aristotle first recorded lucid dreaming in his work entitled "On Dreams." Here he described "being aware" of dreaming while in a dream state. So, how do you know if you have a lucid dream? Here are some pointers:

- You are aware that you are asleep and dreaming

- Your dream is very vivid –like it was actually happening

- You have some kind of control over your dream, including the events and surroundings in your dream

- You feel your emotions intensely

Lucid dreaming enables us to bring our awareness and consciousness into our dreams. When you learn and master the art of lucid dreaming, dreaming does not "happen" to you. You can guide and direct your dreams as they happen. Lucid dreaming is a commonly used Shamanic practice. Experienced Shamans then move on to advanced dreaming techniques, including:

- Bringing their awareness into a dreamless sleep

- Bringing the practice of lucid dreaming into their waking state

Shamans use lucid dreaming from across the globe to convene with others and meet at some point. Crystals are often used to facilitate lucid dreaming for their dream convention. When they compare notes later on, they realize that they did share the same psychic space and can remember what others did and said in the dream meeting. You can use these tips to begin your lucid dreaming journey:

Select a crystal or stone with no sharp edges. You should be able to rub your hands together while holding it.

Before going to bed, set a clear intention for lucid dreaming. You can decide what you want to dream about. It could be anything, including talking to your dead parents, a walk in the mountains, a visit to a school or college to receive training or counseling, etc.

As you focus on your intention, blow onto the stone or crystal in your hand and let your subconscious mind know that it must bring the image of this stone into your dream. Now, hold the stone in your hand.

While you sleep, the stone will fall out of your hand onto your bed. Turn over, lie on it, and again take it into your hand, reaffirming the intention for lucid dreaming.

Keep practicing this, and after a few times, you'll see the stone appear in your dream. You'll realize that you are dreaming while you are in your dream. So, now you are experiencing lucid dreaming. With time and persistent daily practice, you'll be able to guide and direct your dreams to your needs and requirements.

Dream Journaling

What Is a Dream Journal?

A dream journal is like a reflective diary of your dreams. It is a written record of your dreams and your experiences in them. The best and easiest way to start a dream journal is to simply write down what you remember from your dreams. Do not stress yourself about analyzing or interpreting your dreams in the initial stages; just write them down.

In addition to using it for your Shamanic practices, a dream journal can be used to reminisce about important and crucial experiences in your life. So, what are the benefits of dream journaling?

Benefits of Dream Journal

It helps you remember your dreams and improve your overall memory. Dreams are fleeting, and the more you delay recording your dreams from the time of waking up, the less you'll remember. It is best to make entries in your dream journal as soon as you wake up. You'll remember more about it later on when you read your initial musings. The more detailed your dream entries, the more you are exercising your memory muscles.

It improves your understanding of your thoughts and emotions. Dreams affect the way we think and feel. When we wake up from a happy dream, our feelings and thoughts are happy. When we wake up from nightmares, negative emotions drive us crazy. Writing down your dreams helps you understand your feelings and thoughts better. It will help you identify the triggers that brought on the difficult thoughts and emotions, which, in turn, will help you deal with them better.

It improves lucid dreaming ability. Lucid dreaming, as you already know, is a key Shamanic practice. The more you journal about your dreams, the more power you'll have over your lucid dreams. Lucid dreaming helps you delve deep into your subconscious mind, a key quality of a good Shaman.

How to Start and Maintain a Dream Journaling Habit

Don't waste your time waiting for the opportune moment. Just start writing today. Keep that pen and paper next to your bed tonight and start making notes of your dream. Even if you cannot remember a single thing, even then, at least write, "I do not remember my dream."

Putting this thought on paper will trigger something in your subconscious mind, and there will be at least a few elements from your next day's dream that you'll remember. Put that memory on paper immediately. Don't put time between waking up and writing. Do it immediately.

Make your entries as detailed as possible. Ensure you write all details, including:

- The place of the dream.

- Who is or was with you?

- What time was it?

- What was happening?

- What sounds did you hear?

- What colors did you see?

- What emotions did you feel?

Write about all your sensations. In the initial days of dream journaling, you may find it difficult to include all the details. But, with practice, you'll see that your ability to recall every little detail in your dream(s) improves significantly. You should include as many details as possible because these details make it easier to analyze and understand your dreams later on. If you are a good artist, then you can even draw out the scenes you saw in your dreams. Draw and write if you wish, and picture your dreams as vividly as you can.

Compare the events in your dream with the experiences of your waking life. This step is one of the first you can take to try to analyze your dreams. Take your journal with you as you go about your daily work, and write notes about your waking life. Then, write what you saw in your dreams when you wake up the next morning. Are there any similarities? Did something from your waking life trigger your dream that night?

Conversely, did the dream from the previous night trigger any experience in your waking life that day? You can use the old-fashioned paper diary to make your entries, or you can create a soft copy on the computer. There are even mobile apps available for this purpose. You can use any of them. Just start making notes, and you'll be amazed at how much your waking and dreaming lives are intertwined, as any good, experienced Shaman will tell you.

Finally, when you make entries in your dream journal, always use the present tense as if the dream is happening right now. Maintain the present tense even if the images are blurry or unclear. This approach enhances the power of recall. The more you do it, the more in sync your conscious and subconscious mind will be, making remembering dreams easier than before.

Journeying to the Upper World

Journeying to the Upper World is usually done after achieving mastery over basic journeys to the Lower and Middle World. Lucid dreaming, dream journaling, and bringing your dream state into your waking life are all practices that will prepare you for your journeys to the Upper World. Here are a few pointers to help you get started.

Just like how you had a power animal that helped you explore and understand the Lower and Middle Worlds, you'll get one for your travels to the Upper World. It will invariably be a bird, like a hawk or an eagle, with the power to fly high and teach you to look at the bigger picture so that you can put your own life in perspective.

Sit back comfortably in a quiet, undisturbed state. Quieten your mind and get into a state of lucid dreaming if you have mastered that lesson. Make your intention strong about your journey to the Upper World. What do you want to do once you are there? For example, it is usual for Shamans to want to meet their celestial parents in the Upper World for a first journey. We can use this intention for this exercise.

Set your intention to meet with your celestial parents. Close your eyes and imagine the Axis Mundi in front of you, its vast branches and trunk ready to receive you. The roots go deep into the earth. Visualize your astral body traveling up the trunk, or alternatively, imagine walking up a tall ladder placed within the trunk of this tree.

Experience yourself walking up the ladder. Imagine it to be an easy walk as the ladder is vast and comfortable. Visualize reaching the top of the tree and going beyond the clouds. Look around you, find a solid cloud, and place your foot on it. Imagine this cloud floating in the sky and taking you to a doorway at the far end of the sky. Get off from the cloud, approach the door, and knock on it. The gatekeeper will open the door. Seek his permission to enter. State your intention for visiting the Upper World.

When he gives permission to enter, cross over the threshold and wait there. Request the gatekeeper to take you to your celestial parents. As you walk with him on the pathway flanked by light, white clouds, visualize two lights approaching you. As they come close, you'll realize they are your celestial parents, the spirits who do not have form or shape. Speak to them and ask them questions like, "Are you, my celestial parents?" Or "How are you related to me?" Or "Are you my parents?"

As you communicate with the two lights, you'll notice how your thoughts merge with theirs. You realize that you have become one with them, and there is nothing to separate you from them. It is as if they have entered your body and become part of your spirit.

Your celestial parents are the ones who know the true purpose of your life. Ask them what you agreed to be before being born on Earth. Ask them to tell you what the purpose of your spirit was before it merged and gave life to your physical body. What did you come here for? What do you serve?

If you have swayed from the original purpose, request their guidance to help you get back on track. When you have done all that you need to do, thank your celestial parents, and give them permission to go. Ask them for permission to leave also. Accompany the gatekeeper back to the doorway. Climb back on the cloud, waiting on the other side of the doorway, and find your way back to your real home.

When you have finished, slowly become aware of the physical world around you. Open your eyes and notice everything. Move your limbs slowly and get back the sensation of feeling. Take things slowly because it is easy to become disoriented after your first journey to the Upper World. Come back to your real world and bring forth your lessons from above which will help you lead a meaningful, purposeful, authentic life meant for you.

PART THREE: SACRED PLANT ALLIES

Chapter 11: What Are Spirit Plants?

This chapter will give details on using plants as allies or even teachers. In all Shamanic cultures, everything and everyone has inherent medicinal powers which contribute to and help the cosmos in crucial ways. Plants have immense medicinal powers, which are manifested to some energetically powerful people through their combined consciousness.

For example, willow holds the medicine of peace. Even medically speaking, willow is used to make aspirin, a potent pain reliever. Similarly, beech trees hold the medicine of tolerance. The ability to see and feel the medicinal power of plants can be developed if you are willing to go beyond the limitations of the physical dimension. Before we go into the depths of spirit plants, let us explain the concept of plant consciousness in Shamanism.

Shamanism and Plant Consciousness

Human beings lived harmoniously with the plant and animal kingdoms in the ancient world. Shamans regarded plants as aware, sentient, alive, intelligent, and endowed with natural healing powers. Tribal Shamans became powerful spiritual leaders because of their ability to communicate with plants effectively and use their intelligence to learn their healing powers for human use.

The concept of plant spirits has survived since the Stone Age through folklore, rituals, and spiritual teachings passed on orally from teacher to student. The traditional healers of Amazon's Curanderos, present-day folk healers, and even flower essence and homeopathic practitioners believe in the power of plant consciousness.

Nearly all forms of Shamanism spread across the globe believe in the idea that plants can speak to us and give us advice, especially on healing. Plants call us, and we can hear this call if we listen. Here are some pointers on how you can begin working with plants.

• Find Your Plant Ally

The first thing to do is take a trip into the wilderness and meet your plant ally. All you need to do is walk amid nature, keeping your senses open and sharp so that you can receive the messages that plants are trying to send to you. You do not need to find it. Just keep an open mind and take a walk, and your plant will find you.

Before going out on the journey to find your plant ally, set a powerful intention. The energy of your intention will power your journey. This nature trip is all about finding your plant ally, learning about its healing powers, and how it can be put to use to heal the body, mind, and spirit. It is usually considered good, courteous practice to take something to offer the plant as a return gift for its healing powers.

• Shamanic Practice of Gazing at Plants

When you have found your plant ally, or rather when it has found you, spend some time gazing at it. And while you do so, visualize your consciousness merging with that of the plant. With this merging, you'll be able to sense and imbibe the plant's healing powers.

Through diligent practice and by consciously refining and improving our connection with the planet's consciousness, you can cross the boundary separately from the physical world from the higher consciousness realms of plant life. When you cross over to the other side, you can recognize the plant's consciousness and essence and how its healing powers can be imbibed into your soul.

• Treat Plants with Respect and Love

The idea of plant consciousness takes us back to the original Shamanic belief that all things in the cosmos are intertwined with each other, including plant life. Research has shown that plants have emotions, emotions, and intelligence.

A paper published in "Biochemical and Biophysical Research Communications" in July 2021 entitled "Integrated information as a possible basis for plant consciousness" demonstrates that plants, through the evolutionary process, have *"retained a conscious capability even if the strength and size of this ability are yet to be measured and determined."*

Plants can therefore sense our intentions and can respond to our actions. The strength of your intention plays a vital role in awakening the plant spirit of your chosen plant. Also, plants need to be treated with love and respect because they grow and flourish under the influence of these powerful emotions.

Plants are believed to be infinitely compassionate and do not hesitate to call us and dance with us so that their consciousness can be merged with ours, and with this action, their healing powers can be harnessed for our use. We just need to heed their call when they call us.

Vegetalismo Shamans

Vegetalismo refers to "mestizo Shamanism" practiced widely among the tribes of the Peruvian Amazon. Mestizo is a racial classification referring to people with combined European and Indigenous American ancestry. These Shamans are known as "vegetalistas" and gain their Shamanic knowledge and healing skills from the plants of the region, collectively referred to as "vegetales." Many of the vegetalistas imbibe the power from the vegetales by attaining a Shamanic state through the ingestion of ayahuasca, a powerful hallucinogen.

Vegetalistas is a term used to distinguish "plant-powered" Shamans from other healers such as espiritas (spirit healers) and oracionisitas (or prayer healers). Vegetalistas have to prove their worth to the plants before they can obtain healing powers. They undergo severe penance, often going into isolation for six months when they live deep in the wilderness.

During this period of isolation, novices fast for days on end until the plants trust their worth and their true intention to learn from them. They give up sex, oil, fat, and sugar intake and live on extremely limited amounts of food. Mestizo Shamans believe that plants are not fond of the smell emitted by human beings, and so they need to go on fasts to purify themselves so that plants will give permission to come close. This diet is called "La Dieta," during which time they abstain from sex too to get rid of the odor of human sex, which the plant spirits find offensive and vile.

Also, Shamans who need to ingest the plant remain loyal to it while eating it (by ensuring they do not eat anything else). Ingesting into the body allows the plants to teach their healing lessons from within. Shamans take on the smells and powers of the plants they communicate with and imbibe the spirits of the plants.

When neophytes have won the love and trust of the plants, the plant spirits appear to them in their dreams or visions, and that's when they learn the deepest secrets from it, or the icaros (protective, healing songs of the plant). Icaros is a magic melody or chant received as a gift from the plant spirits after winning their love and trust. This song is sung or chanted during the healing ritual, and it belongs only to the healer who has received it directly from the plant.

Vegetalistas also receive other gifts from plants and other senior vegetalistas in their tribe. These powers are given near the end of the completion of the severe penance of fasting and isolation. These powers include:

La Flema – This is a magical saliva-like substance also called "yachay" and represents the concretization of the Shaman's healing power. The La Flema is stored within the Shaman's body. They smoke "mapacho," strong tobacco with high nicotine content, to make the La Flema in their body grow.

Healers also store magic darts (or "virotes") in the La Flema. Virotes are small, poisoned darts that are used as pathogenic projectiles. Some highly powerful Shamans store a rarefied form of virotes called "mariri." Shamans use mariri to extract poisons and sicknesses from patients' bodies. Shamans blow the mariri from their bodies to release its power, which can cure or kill.

Spirit Plants

An interesting question before you learn what a spirit plant is and how to find your spirit plant would be, "How is it possible at all to have spirit plants?" The answer to this question is based on the core Shamanic principle that everything in the cosmos is interconnected. We are all vibrational beings vibrating at different frequencies. Therefore, you can find your vibrational equivalent in any existence. So, just as you found spirit animals, you can find your spirit plants.

Your spirit plant is your plant equivalent, a plant whose spirit vibrates at the same frequency as your spirit. When the two frequencies merge, powerful resonating energy can be put to good and effective use. There are no better or worse spirit plants. Someone with a pink rose plant as their spirit plant is not better or worse than someone whose spirit plant is an oak tree or even some thorny bush. What matters is matching your frequency.

Your spirit plant is the expression of your core essence. It represents your authentic self, and it holds the medicine that you can share with the world. The blueprint of your spirit plant overlaps the blueprint of your life path. Knowing and learning about your spirit plant will help you understand your life purpose and life path and make corrections if you have steered away from it.

A person's outward personality does not always reflect their true essence. Also, self-hate, repressed, unresolved issues lying buried in your subconscious mind, etc., can prevent you from finding your spirit plant. Moreover, the sheer volume and number of plants available on this planet make it very difficult to find your spirit plant.

Therefore, the best way to deal with all these challenges is to work with the idea that you cannot choose your spirit plant, but it can choose you. Since it is a vibrational equivalence of your consciousness, the plant will often turn up in your life, even if you have not stopped to notice it.

So, start with becoming more conscious and aware of the plants in your life. Observe more closely than before the plants and trees that have contributed to your life. Sooner or later, the plant's frequency will connect with yours powerfully, and you'll notice the difference when the connection happens. From your perspective, let go of your ego that prevents your authentic self from making a connection with the spirit plant.

When you have identified your spirit plant, then find out and learn all about it. What are the traits of this plant that match your authentic self? What medicinal powers does the plant hold? Are these powers complementary or aligned with your own? Meditate with the plant. Visualize its growth process and take note of its strengths and weaknesses. Notice if these strengths and weaknesses are reflected in yourself.

Live your life surrounded by things that remind you and keep you connected with your spirit plant. Call upon its energy to awaken you and your Shamanic power. Own the plant's power and medicinal qualities. They are yours for the taking because the plant wants to share them with you. Respect and revere it, and give thanks for being the chosen one.

Totem Plants

Shamans can also have a totem plant which can be a friend, protector, balancer, partner, or guide. Totem plants differ from spirit plants, and you mustn't confuse the two. Normally, an individual's favorite plant becomes their totem plant, whereas a spirit plant vibrates at the same frequency as your spirit.

Shamans, or even non-Shamans, can have multiple totem plants. People wittingly or otherwise tend to their totem plants the most and get maximum physical benefits from them. This happens because the energy flow of totem plants merges with our body and heals every cell and tissue from deep within.

Like spirit plants, finding your totem plants can also be very confusing and mind-boggling. Therefore, it is best to keep your body, mind, and soul open to receive them when they choose you. And yet, you can do some basic exercises to find your totems. Ask yourself these questions:

> • Are there any plants that have always remained in my life, even if I have not really noticed them?

> • Do friends and family always give me a particular plant repeatedly, often without rhyme or reason?

> • Do these plants come up in my life, especially during important milestones?

If any of the above is correct, then the plant may be your totem plant. Sometimes, you can have more than one totem plant. Also, take a walk amid nature and see if you can connect with plants. See if any particular shrub, herb, or tree is calling out to you. Are you drawn to any plant? The outcomes of these exercises are often not immediate. Take your time, be patient, and allow nature to place your totem plants into your life.

Shadow Plants

Shadow plants, also called shadow totem plants, are those that resonate with the frequency of the person's most denied, rejected, and disowned aspect in their consciousness. The same process described under "Spirit Plants" holds good for finding your totem plants and shadow totem plants.

Finding your shadow totem plants requires you to delve deep into your mind and find what aspects of your life you are in denial of or choose to reject. With this information, you can find plants whose properties are connected to these aspects of your life.

The world of Shamanism is rife with stories of how Shamans find their spirit, totem, and shadow plants. Regina's story is one such example. Born and brought up in an urban setting, Regina had very little connection with plants, except the herbs and a few potted indoor plants that her mother had in their little flat in the Bronx, including a little aloe vera pot that was almost hidden behind the bigger ones.

One day, when Regina was about 16, she had a fight with her classmates, a physical fight over some boyfriend issue. She was bruised badly and came home feeling physically, mentally, and emotionally hurt. Her mother had not returned from work, and so she sat alone in her apartment, looking out of the window, tears streaming down her cheeks.

Her bleeding hand was on the sill. Suddenly, she felt a drop of something cold fall onto the wound from out of the blue. She looked down and realized that a drop of sap from the aloe vera plant had fallen. She was quite surprised because it seemed like one little stem of that plant arched over the other plants to allow a drop of healing sap to fall on Regina's hand. The stem looked much longer than the other stems of the plant.

Within an hour, the pain of the bruise reduced considerably, and as if by magic, the next day, her hand was almost completely healed. She was overwhelmed by this episode. She spoke to her mother about it, who gave her a meaningful smile. "I suppose our roots have begun to sprout," she said.

"Don't stop interacting with the aloe vera plant. It is perhaps trying to send you a message," her mother continued. She would sit in front of the aloe vera from that day on and talk to it. She seemed to know how to talk with it, and the plant always responded to her thoughts. This was the start of Regina's journey into Shamanism. Her grandmother and great-grandmother were powerful healers belonging to an ancient Native American tribe. And the aloe vera plant reminded her of this so that she could take the legacy forward.

Chapter 12: Connecting with Plant Allies

So, now that you have identified your spirit, totem, and shadow totem plants, this chapter is dedicated to giving you tips and tricks to establish powerful connections with your plant allies and spirits.

The first doubt that creeps into any novice's brain when communicating with plants is "Can everyone talk to plants?" or "Only those who have achieved high levels of spirituality can do it?" The answer to this is simple. Anyone can talk to and communicate with plants.

Interacting with plant spirits enhances your spirituality. Therefore, those who have achieved high levels of spirituality include exercises of communicating with plants right from the start of their spiritual journey. So, yes, anyone can talk to plants and their spirits, and these interactions deepen your spirituality. An experienced Shaman will find it easier than a beginner to communicate with plants, and that's all there is to it.

The next question for novices is, "Can plants hear us?" And the answer to this is an emphatic yes! They can hear us. You can go back and read about scientific studies mentioned in the previous chapters about plants and their ability to connect with us, feel, and understand. Communicating with plants is done telepathically rather than in the usual fashion that humans do with each other.

Talking to Plant Allies

And remember that you are not talking to the plant body but to its consciousness. This is true when we talk to other people too. We are not talking to the body of the person but to the spirit of the person that makes them alive. In the same way, you are talking to the spirit of the plant.

Therefore, you'll not see mouths moving or facial expressions. But you'll understand their responses and their messages. Talking to plants is a subtle communication system. Often, Shamans hear a voice in their heads, or they may see images, or they may sense a familiar odor, or sometimes, they may get signs and symbols from the plants.

There is nothing complex about talking to your spirit plants. You do not need complex rituals to set up a communication channel between you and your spirit plants. Look at it in this way. Do you have to indulge in complex rituals to talk to your friend, guide, or philosopher? You are likely to set an appointment, even if both of you are busy and you want to have a long conversation about something specific, decide what questions you want to ask them, and then simply go ahead and talk at the appointed time. In fact, if it's your best friend, you may not even need to make an appointment.

The same principle holds good when communicating with your plant spirits. As long as you respect and treat the plant with dignity and honor, you can start communicating with it. For the first conversation, just follow the same etiquette you would follow when you are first speaking to a stranger.

Before starting the conversation with your plant, make sure you find a comfortable, quiet, and undisturbed place. It could be a secluded area in the neighborhood, a quiet spot in the wilderness, etc. Remember to choose a spot where crowds and other noises cannot distract your conversation. Do what works best for you.

You can even do it in the privacy of your home. Remember Regina from the previous chapter? She started her connection with plant spirits in her little flat with the aloe vera plant kept on the small window sill. In fact, you could have a closer connection with house plants because you share living space with them. Your spirits may already have been intertwined with each other. Shamans believe that all plants are alive and have a spirit or consciousness.

Keep a journal to make notes as you converse with your plants. You can use your daily journal or have a special one for this purpose alone.

If you are starting this exercise with a potted plant in your home, you could begin by tidying up the area around the plant, watering it (if needed), or tidying up the soil surface. Perhaps, you can add a layer of new soil to the pot. Show the plant that you care about and love it.

Ask the questions you want to ask. You can talk in your mind or ask your questions out loud. All that matters is to be comfortable and embrace the situation. For example, you could ask a simple question to the plant, "Are you comfortable?" You may or may not hear a clear "yes," or you may get a gut feeling regarding how the plant is feeling.

Give the plant time to respond if you get the feeling that it does not want to talk to you, thank it for giving you the opportunity, and move away. You could come back and try the next day again. You mustn't take the plant's response personally. Remember, not all strangers want to start talking immediately. Some take time to get close. Or it could be that the plant is currently not in the mood to converse.

However, most plants are happy to talk, and they will send you a signal regarding their willingness in some way or another. Even if they do not want to talk, they will listen to your side of the conversation. Mostly, plant spirits are pleasant unless we have done something to hurt them.

If the plant wants to talk (and believe me, you'll know), then sit quietly near the plant and meditate. Clear your mind, connect with your senses. Notice every detail about the plant. Look at the thickness of its stem and branches. Peer at its flowers, See the way it sits in the pot. Notice how the roots are reaching into the soil. Find answers to the following questions:

- What do you feel?

- What do you see?

- What do you hear?

- What can you smell or taste?

Write these answers in your journal. Make notes even if you are in a familiar setting like your home. Writing heightens your ability to sense things. Take permission from the plant to touch it. Wait for its response and then touch it if you get the feeling that it has responded positively to your request. Some simple questions you can ask the plant as you begin your conversation are as follows:

- May I touch you?

- May I sit with you?

The more you dwell on these questions and meditate with them, the deeper your connection with the plants. When you have asked the question, be on alert for signals and signs that the plant is sending you. It could be a vision, or your eyes could fall on an object nearby, and something clicks in your head, and the answer comes to you.

Sometimes, you do not need to ask questions. You can just start talking about yourself. You can tell the plant how much you value it in your life. You can explain why you think plants are important to you. Again, you can have the conversation in your mind or talk to it loudly.

Developing Your Clair Senses

Clair senses are very useful in your ability to build connections with your plant allies. Clair senses are used to communicate with non-human spirits and beings. They can be compared to a different language used by trees and plants to communicate with us. Clair senses are of three primary types:

- **Clairvoyance**

  Clairvoyance is the power of receiving messages as symbols and signs that give you clues to hidden meanings. Clairvoyant people receive visual cues and clues from the plant that's trying to communicate with them. Let us take an example to illustrate this.

  Suppose you ask your plant, "How are you feeling today?" Or, "Do you need anything?" The plant may send you a vision of a lake that you visited a few years ago, or you get a vision of a well. This vision could mean that the plant is asking you to water it. If you are unsure, you can ask a follow-up question like, "Do you need water now?" See what answer you get. Perhaps, the vision of the lake now includes the water coming out into its bank. This could mean that the plant needs the water right now. Keep connecting with the plant and keep looking out for visual cues, and your power of clairvoyance will improve with persistent practice.

- **Clairsentience**

This is a feeling or sensation you get somewhere in your body. If you feel hot or cold without any external or environmental trigger, then this is a message received through the power of your clairsentience. The sensation could be in your gut as well.

For example, if you have asked the plant a question, you could get a warm glow of happiness spreading throughout your body. Depending on your question, you can determine the plant's answer. Sometimes, the sensations and feelings could be very subtle, and sometimes, they could be unusually strong and powerful.

Again, let us take an example to understand how you can interpret the answer. Suppose you ask the plant how it feels, and you feel hot all over your body. It could be that the plant is trying to tell you that it is getting excessive sunlight.

- **Clairaudience**

In this clair sense, you'll get cues through words either in single words or short phrases and sometimes even in full sentences. The more you connect with the plants, and if your clairaudience is well-developed, the more words will flow from the plant's spirit to your consciousness. You can then say these words aloud and record them. You can reflect on these messages to understand what the plant is trying to tell you. Again, do not hesitate to reconfirm your understanding of the plant spirit.

Shamanic Gazing Exercise

The concept of gazing was briefly mentioned in the previous chapter. Here, we shall delve deeper into this Shamanic practice. In Shamanism, gazing is given a lot of importance because it is believed the process of gazing opens our vision to higher dimensions through the increasing frequency of light.

When you gaze steadfastly at something, your speed of awareness becomes so fast that it moves with every moment, helping you remain in the present. At this speed, you are not carrying past baggage nor moving at a pace that goes beyond the present moment. Without the backlog of past perceptions, your behavior changes dramatically.

Gazing at plants is a beautiful journey of falling in love with them and traversing life in their company. Use these steps to gaze at plants and not only build your connection with them but also develop your ability to move into higher dimensions through the power of accurate mindfulness.

- Choose your spirit plant. Place it in front of you at a comfortable angle.

- Sit comfortably and take a couple of deep breaths to clear your mind completely.

- Let your feet touch the ground and realize that it's the same earth on which your plant grows.

- Gaze at your plant with soft, relaxed eyes. Gaze naturally, blinking as usual. Make sure your facial muscles are relaxed. Prepare your mind to gaze and meditate for 10-15 minutes.

- Stare at your plant as if you are seeing it for the first time. Find out what it looks like. Don't label what you see and sense. Just observe.

- Focus on the leaves, stem, roots, and everything else about the plant.

- Notice the unique shapes formed by the various plant parts. Notice how some parts are joined in some places. Notice how other parts are free from all sides except at one point.

- Notice its colors, textures, and fragrances. Feel its energy vibrating with yours.

- You are likely to be distracted by other thoughts. Notice them, do not indulge them, and then let them go. Bring your attention back to your plant.

- When you are satisfied with the gazing experience, thank the plant. Close your eyes and see its image in your inner mind.

- Now, open your eyes and get back your awareness of the surroundings.

Do this gazing exercise as often as you can. You'll notice that your connection with your spirit plants improves considerably.

Chapter 13: Sacred Plants That Heal

This chapter will work as a detailed glossary that looks at Shamans' most important ancient medicinal plants to heal the body and the spirit from negative energies or other spiritual illnesses. It is imperative that before you use any of the medicinal plants mentioned in this chapter to treat any serious illnesses, you must speak to and get approval from a qualified physician.

Medicinal plants and how they are used vary from tribe to tribe. We shall discuss the most popular, accessible, and commonly available plants, especially those used to banish negative energies. Before plucking or harvesting these herbs, you have to ask for permission to do so. This can be done as a prayer or affirmation you can say aloud before plucking the plant part.

Certain plants and herbs have been used to transform and deflect negative energies for centuries now. The reason why this happens is that the plant spirit's vibrational frequency has this power. Here are some of the most common plants whose vibrational powers will help you in your Shamanic journey:

- **Sage**

Sage has been the go-to plant in Shamanism for thousands of years, especially for neutralizing negative energies. The Native Americans of North America have always used the smoke of white sage for cleansing purposes. The smoke emits negative ions and has the same cleansing effects that come after a storm.

Sage leaves are about 2-3 inches long and grow on opposite sides of square-shaped, semi-woody stems. They are oblong and pointed. Sage comes in different colors, including white, blue, purple, black, green, or yellow.

You can apply sage oil to your body before you start a ritual. Apply some to your pulse points to aid with circulation and breathing. Sage can also be burned, and smudging can cleanse you before you enter a trance-like state. Both smudging and applying oil will help to cleanse the energy in your body and the room.

You can gently pass the smudge stick around your body to clear your body's aura of discordant energies. Simply planting sage all around your home will also be hugely beneficial for your entire family. Let us now look at the differences between blue, white, and black sage.

Prayer – *"I call upon the powers of your wondrous energy, O sage, grant me permission to use your powers and guide me so that I may do you no harm."*

- **Blue Sage**

Also called "Grandmother Sage," the blue version is endowed with numerous magical and medicinal benefits. Blue sage is used for purifying and cleansing purposes and is used to provide strength to spiritual practitioners, including Shamans. Blue sage is often used in exorcisms to remove evil spirits. Blue sage is mostly used in a smudge stick with the smoke from the smudging, delivering cleansing and purifying effects.

- **White Sage**

The protective, cleansing, and purifying effects of white sage are legendary and have been harnessed by human beings for thousands of years. Native Americans considered white sage to be sacred. A cleansing and refreshing scent is released when you rub fresh white sage leaves between your thumb and forefinger. The most common way of using white sage is by smudging.

• Black Sage

Black sage promotes dreaming and visioning capabilities. It is used for reflection and introspection. Shamans use black sage for Shamanic journeys and astral projections. When it is burned at night, it aids in restful sleep. It intensifies lucid dreaming and psychic visualization.

• Basil

Basil is known as the plant of love and fertility. Its leaves resemble the shape of a heart. The spirit of the basil plant protects the family. Burning basil oil is a common way used to get rid of negative energies in your home. It is also imbued with the vibrational frequency of happiness, and therefore when you burn basil oil, not only is negative energy eliminated, but positive energy is attracted.

Basil leaves are thick and oblong and have a pointed tip. The leaves grow about 2-4 inches in length and have a glossy-green color. The leaves usually have a slight curve downward with a grooved or bumpy appearance on the surface.

Its vibrational frequency is also connected with sympathy. Therefore, people wear basil for added energy when they know that they may face confrontations, clashes, and conflicts. It is known to clear the connection between your heart and hands, thereby clearing the path to do what your heart wants. Basil is worshiped as a goddess by the Hindus.

Basil can be made into herbal teas. The dried leaves can be included in a smudge stick. You can add it to your ritual bathwater.

Prayer – *"I beseech the vibrational energy of basil to give me permission to pluck a few leaves and use your powers for the good of all."*

• Rosemary

Rosemary is the herb used in love and romance rituals to promote love, relationship longevity, and happiness. The ancient Greeks burned rosemary oil in their temples as offerings to their gods and goddesses. When you burn rosemary essential oil, the negative energies in the surrounding area are eliminated, and everything gets purified and cleansed.

The most common symbolism of rosemary is remembrance, and it is used to enhance your memory power. You can simply sniff the smell of rosemary essential oil to clear your mind and improve your memory.

Rosemary also is associated with passion, friendship, improving sleep, reducing nightmares, etc.

Rosemary can be hung on a doorway for protection. You can add it to your floor and sweep it over the floor to rid your home of negativities. Before performing a ritual, you can use rosemary essential oil to anoint yourself and other magical ingredients.

Leaves of rosemary are long, thin, and needle-like. They start from a quarter of the way up a branch and grow densely. The leaves are dark, greenish-gray in color.

Prayer – *"I beseech the vibrational energy of rosemary to give me permission to pluck a few leaves and use your powers for the good of all."*

• Fennel

Fennel is used to enhance courage, longevity, and strength. Its purifying properties ward off negative energies and protect your aura. It also helps to strengthen your boundaries.

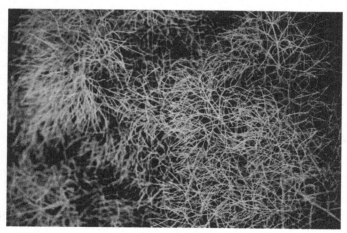

Fennel is the herb of heroes. It is about winning battles and overcoming adversity. Fennel brings vitality, healing, and virility. Fennel plants have gray-green foliage with thread-like leaves. They have the smell of aniseed. Yellow flowers appear at the end of the stems.

Prayer – *"I beseech the vibrational energy of fennel to give me permission to pluck a few leaves and use your powers to thread together love and strength."*

• Sandalwood

Sandalwood is a powerful protector and promotes clairvoyance, divination, and meditation. It is used to build the physical and spiritual well-being of human beings. Sandalwood's vibrational energy can get rid of the distractions in our minds leading us back to the sensual joys offered by our bodies. This oil is used to enhance sexual ecstasy.

Sandalwood vibrates at a frequency that helps to align our chakras. When our chakra system is in balance, we are more open to spiritual energies. When this happens, healing energies flow unhindered right through our body and mind.

Sandalwood is fine-grained, heavy, and yellow in color. They are aromatic and retain their fragrance for decades. Sandalwood oil is extracted from the woods and stems of sandalwood trees.

Prayer – *"I beseech the vibrational energy of sandalwood to give me permission to extract your essential oil and use your powers for protection and well-being."*

• Ylang-Ylang

Ylang-ylang is the perfect aid for all rituals dealing with love, sex, and peace. Its vibrational energies and fragrance have soothing, calming effects and are specifically useful in negative situations. When used correctly with powerful visualization techniques, ylang-ylang can be an excellent aphrodisiac.

Ylang-ylang is a star-shaped, yellow flower native to the countries around the Indian Ocean, including Malaysia, the Philippines, India, and Indonesia. They have a head, aromatic, fruity, and flowery smell.

Prayer – *"I beseech the vibrational energy of ylang-ylang to give me permission to use your powers for love and peace."*

- **Eucalyptus**

The power of eucalyptus lies in its ability to clear negative psychic energy in the surroundings. This herb and its essential oil are often used for this purpose in physical, emotional, and verbal combat situations. It carries the energy needed to cleanse your path of all negativities. It is also used to clear out residual energies after rituals.

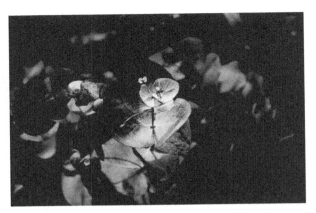

Eucalyptus trees are evergreen with lanceolate-shaped leaves that have a glossy green appearance. However, there are many varieties of eucalyptus trees with varying shapes and sizes.

Prayer – *"I beseech the vibrational energy of eucalyptus to give me permission to pluck a few leaves and use your powers for protection against negative psychic energies."*

• Vetiver

Vetiver strengthens our energetic boundaries to keep out negative energies from invading our aura. It increases the flow of vital energy in our body and is great for grounding and stabilizing our physical and emotional bodies. Vetiver's energy manifests psychic protection, tranquility, centering, wisdom, peace, intuition, and luck.

Prayer – *"I beseech the vibrational energy of vetiver to give me permission to pluck a few leaves and use your powers for the good of all."*

• Oregano

Oregano is the herb of love and harmony. It is beneficial in Shamanic practices as it helps with balance and harmony, allowing you to become settled as you enter a trance. Its medicinal properties have been harnessed since ancient times. Oregano not only helps with spiritual balance but with physical balance too, and is often used to treat physical ailments.

Brewing a tea with oregano will result in not only medicine that can be consumed but also a vapor that removes negativity from the air.

Prayer – *"I beseech the vibrational energy of oregano to give me permission to pluck a few leaves and use your powers for harmony and happiness."*

• Lavender

Lavender is the go-to plant for all rituals dealing with peace, love, and health. Its vibrational frequency has the power to dispel depression and anxiety. It also helps us to keep our emotions in check. If you have sleeplessness issues at night, you can sprinkle a bit of lavender essential oil on your pillow to promote sleep.

Lavender is the herb of devotion. You can harness it to improve focus and dedication when performing rituals. Lavender can be used as an essential oil, powders, and in ritual baths.

Prayer – *"I beseech the vibrational energy of lavender to give me permission to pluck a few leaves and use your powers for a good night's sleep."*

- **Frankincense**

Frankincense is a powerful tool to achieve a heightened state of spiritual awareness. When you use frankincense, you awaken your spiritual side. This is because the herb is about love and connection. It is a calming herb that allows you to tap into your sensitive nature that loves itself and others.

It is a powerful protector and purifier of negative energies. It promotes inner peace.

Prayer – *"I beseech the vibrational energy of frankincense to give me permission to use your powers to improve spiritual awareness."*

- **Rue**

Rue is best known for its powers of spiritual cleansing and can keep out negative vibes from envy and bad luck. In the Middle Ages, rue was hung on the doorways to keep out evil spirits. It was known as the "herb of grace," and churches used it to sprinkle holy water on worshippers.

It works best when you burn rue on charcoal tablets. When the charcoal tablet is heated and ready, sprinkle small amounts of rue to release smoke slowly and without a flame. You can then take the charcoal tablet all around the designated space (either your home or a ritual space) for the smoke to purify and cleanse every nook and cranny.

Prayer – *"I beseech the vibrational energy of rue to give me permission to pluck a few leaves and use your powers for the good of all."*

Chapter 14: Magical Plants to Enhance Sight

This chapter will be dedicated to ancient medicinal plants that have been used to induce trances so that journeying can happen with more ease. It is imperative to remember that this book does not promote the use of psychoactive plants without strict supervision by trained and experienced practitioners. This book only gives an indication of the insight-enhancing powers of plants. Please use them only under the supervision of reputable, experienced practitioners.

Ayahuasca

Stories of travelers and tourists going to different exotic foreign locations to take part in the Ayahuasca ceremony are rife on the Internet. When administered wrongly, Ayahuasca, a psychoactive brew, can result in dangerous and certainly avoidable situations. However, when done correctly and administered in accurate doses under the strict supervision of experienced Shamans, then ayahuasca can take you on Shamanic journeys and to altered states of consciousness from where you can access the astral realms.

Ayahuasca is known as "the tea" and is brewed with the leaves of the Psychotria Viridis plant combined with the stalks of the Banisteriopsis caapi vine. While these are the two primary ingredients that go into the Ayahuasca, other ingredients and plants could also be added depending on the Shaman's and/or the seeker's needs.

A highly experienced Shaman always leads an authentic Ayahuasca ceremony. The Shaman boils the leaves and the stalks in water. The leaves are simply torn and added, whereas the vine is cut up and crushed before being added to extract its medicinal properties optimally.

When the brew is ready, the Shaman removes the water and repeats the process until a concentrated thick brew is produced. When the brew cools down completely, the impurities are strained out. As a prerequisite to participating in an Ayahuasca ceremony, you must abstain from alcohol, sex, drugs, cigarettes, and caffeine, preparing and purifying your body. Many Shamans also recommend following a strict diet, veganism or vegetarianism, to ensure that all toxins are removed from your body before the ceremony.

The ceremonies are always held at night under the strict supervision of an experienced Shaman who watches every participant closely for any adverse effects. The ceremony lasts until the effects of the Ayahuasca wear off from all the participants. The ritual space is prepared, cleaned, and purified through smudging and other rituals. The leading Shaman blesses it.

Then, the Ayahuasca brew is served to the participants, usually in small, numerous doses. After consumption, the effects begin about 20-60 minutes later and last about 2-6 hours, depending on the dose taken and the personal health condition of the participant. For novices, the unpleasant but normal symptoms are vomiting and diarrhea.

The Shamanic preparations are not as simplistic as mentioned above. They are complex processes done with accurate doses of various substances, the outcome of which can result in powerful visions. The other reactions, including auditory and visual hallucinations, feelings of euphoria, fear, paranoia, and mind-altering psychedelic effects, are person-specific.

Some people experience feelings of enlightenment and euphoria, while others might experience fear and paranoia. Some experience extreme anxiety and panic too. Nearly every participant feels both positive and negative effects from the brew. The Shamans and their teams monitor the ceremony closely and have medical staff close by to handle emergencies, if any. The benefits of ayahuasca are:

- The active ingredients in ayahuasca, namely DMT and β-carbolines, have demonstrated the power to protect and restore neurons. Some other ingredients help protect brain cells too.

- It improves psychological well-being by promoting mindfulness, emotional regulation, and enhancing mood.

To reiterate vital information, ayahuasca should NOT be taken without the strict supervision of experienced and reputed Shamans.

Peyote

Peyote is a hallucinogenic plant native to Mexico. The indigenous Huichol tribe considers this plant sacred. The Huichol people have protested against its indiscriminate use by uninformed, insensitive travelers and scammers. Peyote's healing effects have been used since around 300 BCE. It is used in folklore medicine to treat intestinal disorders, influenza, consumption, arthritis, scorpion, and snake bites, and as an antidote for datura poison.

Peyote is a dome-shaped, spineless cactus plant with button-like nodules. These are found throughout the Chihuahuan Desert from Mexico to Texas. Its primary active chemical is mescaline. Fresh or dried nodules are either chewed or boiled with water to make a bitter brew. The "trip" after consuming peyote usually lasts 6-12 hours.

Peyote has been used for centuries by Shamans, medicine men, and indigenous tribes of North America. The Shamans ingest peyote to communicate with the spirit world and to undertake Shamanic journeys.

A growing body of research work now appears to prove that peyote has multiple health benefits, which the Shamans of the region have known for thousands of years. Like all sensitive plants, peyote also needs to be used only under the strict monitoring of experienced Shamans. The health benefits of peyote are:

- Peyote stimulates spiritual experiences. It is known to induce states of deep insight and trigger psychoactive experiences. Users have reported symptoms of synesthesia, an uncommon sensation wherein one stimulus automatically triggers another reaction. For example, if you hear a sound (the stimulus), you see a vision of colors (reaction).

- Peyote is known to help improve problem-solving skills. Thanks to the presence of multiple psychoactive alkaloids, specifically mescaline, peyote is believed to improve creative problem-solving capabilities.

- Peyote improves feelings of happiness. It is known to activate serotonin receptors which, in turn, has a positive impact on perceptions and moods.

Peyote is a controlled substance in North America, and its use is restricted to Native American ceremonies under the supervision of experienced Shamans.

Psychoactive Fungi

Psychoactive fungi are of numerous types, including psilocybin mushrooms or magic mushrooms and various Amanita mushrooms. Magic mushrooms are available in the wild and may be cultivated too. They contain psilocybin, a natural hallucinogenic and psychoactive substance. In the US, psilocybin is categorized as a Schedule I drug, which means it is highly prone to be misused.

Psychoactive fungi can be mixed with food, brewed like tea, or eaten as it is. They can also be smoked, usually mixed with cannabis or tobacco. These mushrooms are hallucinogenic, which means when you ingest them, you can hear, feel, and see things and sensations that are not real.

Shamans in indigenous tribes of Europe and North America have used these fungi for spiritual and medicinal purposes for thousands of years. Psychoactive fungi have a long history of association with self-discovery and spiritual experiences. Shamans use psychoactive fungi to attain altered and higher levels of consciousness.

Consuming magic mushrooms usually results in a mild "trip" where you can feel drowsy or relaxed. However, some people do have frightening experiences like paranoia, severe panic, and delusions. It is also known to cause convulsions in rare and extreme cases. The physical effects of consuming magic mushrooms are dilated pupils, headaches, drowsiness, increased heart rate, temperature, and blood pressure, muscle weakness, lack of coordination, yawning, and nausea.

Mental effects of psychoactive fungi are euphoria, distorted sense of reality, visual and/or auditory hallucinations, powerful spiritual experiences, paranoia, panic reactions, and sometimes, even psychosis.

The most well-known Amanita mushroom is the fly agaric mushroom. It has been used in the Shamanic world for centuries to commune with the spiritual world. It grows to about 8-20 cm in diameter with an orange-red to the orange-scarlet cap. The fly agaric is one of the earliest known hallucinogens used by indigenous tribes and Shamans to achieve Shamanic states and undertake journeys to the three worlds discussed earlier in the book.

Shamans used fly agaric mushrooms to mentally "fly" to higher states of consciousness and speak to, get advice, and bring back messages from spirit guides and higher realm beings. Reindeers in northern Europe are drawn to fly agaric mushrooms. The Siberian people will look out for reindeers exhibiting intoxicated behaviors, slaughter them, and eat their meat to feel the same intoxication.

The hallucinogenic ingredient passes out of the body via the urine of the person who has ingested the mushroom. Therefore, Shamans often ate the mushrooms (because they had the power to withstand its powerful hallucinogenic effects), and the rest of the tribespeople would drink the Shaman's urine. An earlier chapter described the connection with fly agaric, Shamans, and Santa Claus.

This exercise may seem revolting by modern standards. However, if the Shaman has fasted (as required before any Shamanic state ritual), the urine will contain nothing more than water mixed with the hallucinogenic compound. Also, the fly agaric mushroom was dried out or made into a thin tea or soup to reduce the toxic effects of the hallucinogen.

And finally, it is imperative to remind you again that you should only attempt to try these plants in a controlled setting and under the supervision of an experienced Shaman.

Chapter 15: Shamanic Rituals and Practices

This chapter is dedicated to giving you as many Shamanic rituals and practices as are needed by novices to begin their sojourn into the world of Shamanism.

How to Prepare a Shamanic Bath

We are continuously interacting with different people and situations and imbibing all kinds of energies from them, both directly and indirectly. Additionally, we are also sending out energy vibrations in all directions through our interactions involving thoughts, emotions, and words.

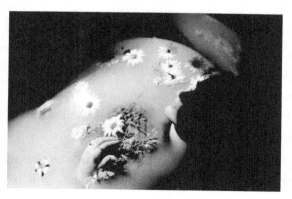

This relentless interaction of our energy force with those of others drains our aura, which is continuously adjusting on its own and trying to regain its original harmony. While our aura can readjust on its own, often accumulated negative energy becomes so powerful that it can linger on for inconveniently long periods. As a budding Shaman, you must regularly work to clear and cleanse your aura. One of the best ways to do this is the Shamanic or spiritual bath.

So, how different is a Shamanic bath from a normal bath? Regular baths are specifically used for cleansing the physical body. While we get some sense of calm and peace after a regular bath, the primary purpose is to maintain physical body hygiene. On the other hand, spiritual baths are rituals intended for spiritual cleansing and hygiene. A spiritual bath cleanses your subtle energy bodies and your aura and revitalizes your subtle senses. After a spiritual bath, you'll feel completely rejuvenated, refreshed, and have a deep sense of inner peace.

Another important difference between a regular bath and a spiritual one is the time taken. Regular baths usually take about 10 to 20 minutes. A spiritual bath can take anywhere between 20 and 60 minutes. So, before you begin the bath, make sure you have dedicated yourself to an uninterrupted period of an hour. Then follow these steps:

Set the space for the bath. Ensure it is totally clean and hygienic. Your bathtub, countertops, and entire bathroom should be clean and organized. Clear all clutter. Also, make space for the various things you'll need for the ritual. Pick the crystals, stones, flowers, herbs, essential oils, etc., with an intended purpose.

Choose the scent of your candles or essential oils that are aligned with your feelings. There are no right or wrong decisions to make. Select what you believe will soothe you.

Then, choose a sound to play. Calm meditative music or even gentle, rhythmic drumming or binaural beats will work wonders.

Loud and/or lyrical music should be avoided as the words may hinder your thought process of clearing your aura.

The following ingredients will be needed:

1. **Baking soda** – Baking soda releases bicarbonate and sodium ions when dissolved in water, which offers numerous health and spiritual cleansing benefits. You can use about ¼- 2 cups of it, depending on the size of your bathtub.

2. **Salt** – natural salt is a great cleansing agent and can clear any lingering negative energies from your auric field. Natural sea salt, Epsom salt, or pink Himalayan salt are excellent choices. About 2-3 handfuls would be more than enough. Do not use table salt used in cooking because it is artificially refined and contains anti-caking agents.

3. **Crystals** – Crystals have their own healing properties depending on their vibrational energies. Choose those crystals that are aligned with your intention. For example, Celestite is to reduce stress; rose quartz is to attract love, etc.

4. **Lavender** – You can use whole buds that are boiled in water to extract the aroma, or you can drop enough of the essential oil to get the aroma you want. Lavender calms your mind and emotions. It is an excellent stress buster.

5. **Essential Oils** – Some believe that the vibrational frequencies of essential oils are the closest to that of human beings. Each essential oil affects your senses in different ways. Sandalwood is for focus (a ritual bath with sandalwood before undertaking Shamanic journeys will be hugely beneficial). Peppermint energizes and gets rid of fatigue.

1. Other flowers and herbs that can add value to your Shamanic bath are:

- **Rosewater** – Boil fresh pink or red rose petals until they lose all their color. Add this water to a warm bath. Rose uplifts your moods and promotes self-love. You can also add fresh or dried petals directly into the bathwater for added aroma.

- **Carnations** – Boil red and pink carnations with honey and coconut milk in water. Strain it and add the water to your bath. Carnations are excellent to soothe sadness and depression. It also helps heal a broken heart.

- Herbs of your choice. You can refer to Chapter 13 for healing plants and choose from the list given there.

If you do not have the time to prepare the ingredients for your bath, then you can pick up readymade spirit bath sets from online stores and use them according to the instructions given in the package. To reiterate, remember to set a clear intention for your ritual bath. For example:

- This ritual bath will clear and cleanse my aura of all negativities.

- This spiritual bath will focus my mind on the Lower World journey.

- This Shamanic bath is my weekly cleansing and protecting ritual.

The Sun Ritual

The Sun Ritual or the Sun Dance is one of the most powerful ancient Shamanic rituals that has survived the tides and beatings of time and multiple bans brought about by seemingly advanced modern countries. This dance originated among the indigenous tribes of North America.

This unique ritual was conducted every summer and was primarily dedicated to celebrating the Earth and the Sun. However, each individual dancer danced for their private wishes and desires. They could partake in the dance, asking for a better future for their family, improved health, or find their life purpose, etc.

The musical instruments involved were drums and ceremonial pipes. It was a long and grueling dance that lasted an entire day and often flowed into the night as well. They were trance-like ceremonies where the fit and young members of the tribes pierced their own bodies as a form of sacrifice to show their respect and love for the endurance of the Sun and Earth. The self-inflicted piercings were the primary reasons for the ban.

However, modern members of Native American tribes still perform the dance, all the while trying to demystify its secrets and portraying it as a safe and celebratory ritual. They use the power of the Sun to get rid of their pain and difficulties and imbibe it into their lives. From a modern Shamanic perspective, here is what you can do as a simple, daily sun ritual:

- Just before sunset, go outside and face the direction of the setting sun.

- Say aloud, *"O Sun God, I surrender all my worries and fears to you. Dispel and eliminate them in your burning fire."*

- The next morning, just before sunrise, go outside and face the direction of the rising sun.

- Say aloud, *"O Sun God, upon rising on a new day, give me new, refreshing strength from your burning fire."*

Invoking the Elements

Invoking the power and energies of the four elements is one of the most common pre-ceremony Shamanic rituals. The energies of the elements are invoked and invited into the sacred space before a ritual. At the end of the ritual, thanks and permission to leave are given to the elements. You can use the following pointers to invoke the elements:

Turn to the east, which represents the air element, and say, *"With an open heart, we call upon the guardians of the east and the powers of air and wind to come and participate in our ritual. Protect and keep us safe. We pray to the winds of inspiration. We pray for the power of comprehension and understanding. We thank you for the breath of life that you bestow upon us every waking moment."*

Turn to the south representing the fire element, and say, *"With an open heart, we call upon the guardians of the south and the powers of fire to come and participate in our ritual. We pray for the strength to explore our creativity. We pray for the passion of the burning fire. We thank you for the sparks of life."*

Turn to the west representing the water element, and say, *"With an open heart, we call upon the guardians of the west and the powers of water to come and participate in our ritual. Water surrounds us from the time of being in our mother's wombs. You are there in the blood in our veins, in tears in our eyes. We pray that you cleanse us with your purity. We honor and thank you for your flowing presence."*

Turn to the north representing the earth, and say, *"With an open heart, we call upon the guardians of the north and the powers of the earth to come and participate in our ritual. You bestow us with numerous gifts. You give birth to new life. You nourish and nurture our bodies. Teach us to dance gently on your sacred land, and teach us the humility you spread. Thank you for your solid support."*

Practice the above Shamanic rituals as often as you can. The more you practice, the deeper the essence of the practice will get into your unconscious mind. Consequently, your way of life will transform from an ordinary one to a Shamanic one.

Extra: Daily Shamanic Transformation

This last part of the book represents a 2-week calendar with a few recommended Shamanic practices to try every day.

1. Remember, you are connected to the entire cosmos. You have the inherent power to simply close your eyes and harness the energy surrounding you. You also should know that what you do reflects in the cosmos. Imagine a cord from your belly button connecting to every other cord that emanates in this cosmos.

2. Sit quietly. Close your eyes and imagine this cord extending deep into the earth. Imagine it growing upwards too and disappearing into the vastness of the sky. Visualize light coming from the two directions and entering your body, rejuvenating and refreshing you. You also send out feelings of love and compassion back to the cosmos.

3. Remember your thoughts and emotions are connected because Shamans know that the body, mind, and spirit are intimately intertwined with each other. This means your thoughts create your emotions and your emotions create your thoughts. Pay attention to this connection.

4. The next time you feel happy, focus on the thought that's in your mind. What thought is triggering the emotion of happiness? In the same way, when you have a troubling or disturbing thought causing you heartache, focus on the emotion that's causing you pain. A simple shift in thought can shift your emotions too.

5. When you feel sad, think of a happy situation, and the sadness will be replaced with joy. If you feel overwhelmed, you might get the thought, "What am I going to do with this?" Catch the thought and let it go, and the feeling will follow it too. Keep practicing on this thought-emotion connection activity, and soon you'll find it easy to manage your emotions maturely, one of the first tests leading to Shamanic wisdom.

6. Remember to respect the Earth. Shamanism is deeply associated with Mother Nature and Mother Earth. Earth or Gaia supports all life forms, and it is imperative to give her the respect she deserves for this. Say a daily prayer for her well-being. Sing a song every day. Tend a garden. Remember to recycle and reuse and not burden Mother Earth with our trash.

7. Reach out for the power and energy of the four elements. Use the prayers given in the previous chapter and call out for help to the four elements, including earth, air, fire, and water. Earth is excellent for grounding and stability. Water is great for letting go. Allow your problems and fears

to flow away as water does. Fire is excellent to release deep-seated problems. Burn them away from the roots ensuring they never return to harass you. Air is great for clearing negative energies. Call the power of the air element to clear away negativity from your life.

8. Pay attention to plants and animals. In Shamanism, medicine is anything that heals, nurtures, and nourishes your body, mind, and spirit. Healing can come in any form, including the love from a pet, the scent of a plant, a kind word from a stranger, and of course, from simple and elaborate healing rituals.

9. Animals and plants carry medicine for you. If you see an animal or a plant crossing your path or appearing in your dreams frequently, then pay attention to it. Open your senses and look out for messages the plant or animal is trying to send to you. Messages could be in the form of a visual sign or signal.

10. Practice being a jaguar or an eagle. Eagles and jaguars are powerful Shamanic symbols. As you already know, jaguars are not considered to be just animals. They are believed to be spirits of experienced Shamans who have passed on and want to walk the surface of the Earth they once lived in.

11. Also, being a jaguar gives you practice in stealth and patience. He walks through the jungle, noticing and observing everything and missing nothing. In the same way, lead your life, ensuring you notice, observe, and imbibe everything around you. Keep your senses sharp and alert. This approach builds your inner Shamanic power and instincts.

12. Being an eagle reminds you to get the bigger picture and not to be concerned about the little things that do not really make any difference in the larger perspective. For example, if your child is creating problems, be like an eagle, and show compassion and love by stepping back from the scene. Like the eagle, wait for the right time to do what needs to be done. Soar into the clouds and avoid getting caught in the drama and heat of that moment.

13. Do some little ritual every day. It could be a simple "me-time" self-healing ritual where you find a quiet spot in your home, get a few minutes of undisturbed time, sit with your favorite crystals or herbs or essential oils, invoke the elements, and ask for healing. Add the simple sun ritual described in the previous chapter into your daily routine.

14. Create an altar. An altar reminds you of your chosen Shamanic path. Create a simple altar that could become your healing space. It could even be a corner of your worktable. Arrange your favorite pieces of art, idols, crystals, candles, etc. Light a candle every day in this space, ensuring that all aspects of fire safety are taken care of.

Start with any of the tips given in this chapter. Practice it diligently for two days. When you are comfortable, add a second one, then a third one, and so on. Apart from the altar building, there are seven simple exercises to bring about a complete Shamanic transformation in your life, with two days for each task.

While we do call it a 2-week calendar, it is important to remember that results can vary.

Some of you may be able to get into the routine of daily Shamanic transformation in 2 weeks, while others may have to repeat it a couple of times or more before mastering it. There is no right or wrong way of doing this. There is no one judging you. Do it at the pace that you are most comfortable with and without rushing through it.

Conclusion

To conclude this exhaustive, informative book, let us look again at the philosophy of Shamanism. According to this ancient, far-reaching belief system, all things in this cosmos are manifestations of the Spirit, which, in turn, is present in all things. Everything is alive, and everything is interconnected and interrelated with each other.

Shamans do not see human beings as the pinnacle of evolution. They see dynamic relationships intertwining mutual responsibility that bind everything in this cosmos, including human, non-human, living, and non-living things. Shamanic practices and rituals aim to recognize, restore, and honor these deeply intertwined and interlaced relationships.

Leading a personal Shamanic way of life builds wondrous habits that help you connect with Mother Nature, Mother Earth, the four elements, and all creatures of this world. The deeper you delve into your soul, the stronger your Shamanic way of life will become. Start with the simple understanding that we are all interconnected. Our actions send ripples across the cosmos affecting everything else in it, just as every action of others sends ripples back to us, affecting us and our lives.

The interconnectedness can cause conflict or harmonious living. The way of Shamanism chooses the latter because it is far more powerful and productive than conflicts.

Here's another book by Silvia Hill that you might like

Free Bonus from Silvia Hill available for limited time

Hi Spirituality Lovers!

My name is Silvia Hill, and first off, I want to THANK YOU for reading my book.

Now you have a chance to join my exclusive spirituality email list so you can get the ebooks below for free as well as the potential to get more spirituality ebooks for free! Simply click the link below to join.

P.S. Remember that it's 100% free to join the list.

~~$27~~ FREE BONUSES

- ❦ 9 Types of Spirit Guides and How to Connect to Them
- ❦ How to Develop Your Intuition: 7 Secrets for Psychic Development and Tarot Reading
- ❦ Tarot Reading Secrets for Love, Career, and General Messages

Access your free bonuses here
https://livetolearn.lpages.co/sh-shamanism-paperback/

Index of Terms

Medicine Wheel – Since ancient times, the medicine wheel has been used for healing and healthy purposes by Indigenous tribes, especially among Native American tribes.

Shamanic Journeying – Shamanic journeying is when a Shaman undertakes a journey through their mind into the three primary worlds, namely the Lower World, the Middle World, and the Upper World. The Shaman undertakes these journeys into the Lower, Middle, and Upper Worlds through an altered state of consciousness.

Lower World – This is the world of raw potential and the place you go to for healing, soul-searching, and soul repair.

Middle World – This is a reflection of the physical world along with hidden and unseen beings and spirits.

Upper World – This is the realm of the Spirit where celestial beings reside.

Plant Allies – Every Shaman has plant allies that help, guide, and act as mentors in their Shamanic path.

Animal Allies – Every Shaman has animal allies that guide and mentor them, especially during Shamanic journeys.

Ayahuasca - The Ayahuasca ceremony is practiced among the vegetalistas and is used for healing and cleansing purposes. Today, tourists from all over the world travel to Peru to participate in Ayahuasca ceremonies where they ingest ayahuasca (in controlled quantities) depending on what they are seeking. They may also seek to cure illnesses and sometimes even to purge and cleanse themselves. The touristy ceremony is usually done in an urban setting conducted by a vegetalismo Shaman. However, the rural settings of Ayahuasca ceremonies are quite different. Among the tribes, people involved in the ceremony are family and kindred people, whereas, in the urban setting, strangers from different parts of the world sit together.

References

'- INVOCATION for OPENING SACRED SPACE.' The Four Winds, 26 June 2015, thefourwinds.com/blog/Shamanism/opening-sacred-space

'-the Shaman's Tools.' The Four Winds, 31 Jan. 2017, thefourwinds.com/blog/Shamanism/the-Shamans-tools

' – DRAWING LIFE from YOUR DREAMS – a SHAMANIC EXERCISE.' The Four Winds, 9 Apr. 2019, thefourwinds.com/blog/Shamanism/drawing-life-dreams-Shamanic-exercise

' – Journey to the Upper World.' The Four Winds, 19 May 2020, thefourwinds.com/blog/Shamanism/journey-upper-world/.

' – PREPARING to JOURNEY to the LOWER WORLD.' The Four Winds, 12 Nov. 2019, thefourwinds.com/blog/Shamanism/preparing-journey-lower-world

' – RETRIEVING YOUR POWER ANIMAL.' The Four Winds, 3 Mar. 2020, thefourwinds.com/blog/Shamanism/retrieving-power-animal

'9 Ways to Use Shamanism in Your Everyday Life | Meghan Gilroy.' Www.meghangilroy.com, 28 Mar. 2015, www.meghangilroy.com/9-practical-ways-to-use-Shamanism-in-your-everyday-life

12 Plants & Herbs to Transform Negative Energy – EVERYTHiNG SOULFuL. everythingsoulful.com/12-plants-herbs-transform-negative-energy

'30 Sacred Herbs for Smudging and Cleansing Purposes.' Ilmypsychicjane, www.ilmypsychicjane.com/single-post/2017/12/09/30-Sacred-Herbs-for-Smudging-and-Cleansing-Purposes

'A Middle World Journey for Finding Your Anchor Spot!' Shaman's Way, 9 May 2015, Shamansway.net/middle-world-journey

'About Sacred Herbs & Smudging Ceremonies | How to Smudge | Incense Resins.' Www.taosherb.com, www.taosherb.com/store/sacred-herbs.html

'An Intro to Flower Gazing Meditation.' Garden Collage Magazine, 13 Feb. 2017, gardencollage.com/heal/mind-spirit/intro-flower-gazing-meditation

'Article: Opening the Doors to the Self – the Shamanic Journey.' Sacred Stream, 21 Oct. 1998, www.sacredstream.org/opening-the-doors-to-the-self-the-Shamanic-journey-3

Calvo, Paco, et al. 'Integrated Information as a Possible Basis for Plant Consciousness.' Biochemical and Biophysical Research Communications, Oct. 2020, 10.1016/j.bbrc.2020.10.022

'Can You Learn to Lucid Dream?' Verywell Mind, www.verywellmind.com/what-is-a-lucid-dream-5077887

'DailyOM – Shamanic Journeying by Sandra Ingerman.' Www.dailyom.com, www.dailyom.com/cgi-bin/display/librarydisplay.cgi?lid=2592

Daley, Kathleen. 'Plant Spirit Shamanism: Hearing the Call of the Plants.' Blog.pachamama.org, blog.pachamama.org/plant-spirit-Shamanism-call-plants

Drake, Michael. 'Shamanic Drumming: Crafting a Shamanic Drum.' Shamanic Drumming, 29 Mar. 2012, Shamanicdrumming.blogspot.com/2012/03/crafting-Shamanic-drum.html

Dresler, Martin, et al. 'Volitional Components of Consciousness Vary across Wakefulness, Dreaming and Lucid Dreaming.' Frontiers in Psychology, vol. 4, 2014, 10.3389/fpsyg.2013.00987

Finding Your Plant Totem | Wishing Moon. wishingmoon.com/finding-your-plant-totem

Fly agaric Amanita Muscaria Magic Mushroom – Shamanic Journey. www.Shamanicjourney.com/fly-agaric-amanita-muscaria-magic-mushroom

Gingras, Bruno, et al. 'Exploring Shamanic Journeying: Repetitive Drumming with Shamanic Instructions Induces Specific Subjective Experiences but No Larger Cortisol Decrease than Instrumental Meditation Music.' PLoS ONE, vol. 9, no. 7, 7 July 2014, p. e102103, 10.1371/journal.pone.0102103

Hartney, Elizabeth. 'What to Know about Magic Mushroom Use.' Verywell Mind, Verywell Mind, 26 Feb. 2012, www.verywellmind.com/what-are-magic-mushrooms-22085

'How a Shaman Rattle Is Made.' Www.beardrum.com, www.beardrum.com/rattleconstruction.html

'Mindbodygreen.' Mindbodygreen, 17 May 2017, www.mindbodygreen.com/articles/how-to-find-your-spirit-animal

'What Is Animism?' Learn Religions, 2019, www.learnreligions.com/what-is-animism-4588366

Huels, Emma R., et al. 'Neural Correlates of the Shamanic State of Consciousness.' Frontiers in Human Neuroscience, vol. 15, 18 Mar. 2021, 10.3389/fnhum.2021.610466

incahealinggoddess. 'Mesa Carrier.' Incahealinggoddess, 3 Mar. 2016,

incahealinggoddess.wordpress.com/2016/03/03/mesa-carrier

'Is Holotropic Breathwork Right for You?' Verywell Mind, www.verywellmind.com/holotropic-breathwork-4175431

Joseph, Bob. 'What Is an Indigenous Medicine Wheel?' Www.ictinc.ca, 24 May 2020, www.ictinc.ca/blog/what-is-an-indigenous-medicine-wheel

'Lucid Dreaming.' Corrosion-Doctors.org, 2014,

www.corrosion-doctors.org/Dreaming%20is%20Personal/Lucid.htm

'Make Your Own Smudge Sticks to Banish Bad Energy.' Hello Nest, 13 Oct. 2020, hellonest.co/diy-smudge-sticks/.

'Medicine Bundle Meaning & Step Builder.' Www.sacredessence.co.uk,

www.sacredessence.co.uk/medicine-bundle-meaning-step-builder-i78

'Medicine Wheel: How I Use Its Teachings in My Healing Journey.' Healthy Debate, 3 Oct. 2018, healthydebate.ca/2018/10/topic/medicine-wheel

NativeAmericanVault.com. 'Totem Animals and Their Meanings.' NativeAmericanVault.com, www.nativeamericanvault.com/pages/totem-animals-and-their-meanings

'Penzu.' Penzu, penzu.com/dream-journal.

Peyote Visions and Alternate Reality – Shamanic Journey. www.Shamanicjourney.com/peyote-visions-and-alternate-reality

PhD, Daniel Foor. Ancestral Medicine: Rituals for Personal and Family Healing. Amazon, Bear & Company, 11 July 2017, www.amazon.in/dp/B01MFFK2OM/ref=dp-kindle-redirect?_encoding=UTF8&btkr=1

'Psychics & Mediums Share 7 Tips for Traveling to Other Realms.' Bustle, www.bustle.com/life/astral-projection-techniques-explore-astral-realm-psychics-mediums

'Rattle Medicine.' Www.soundtravels.co.uk, www.soundtravels.co.uk/a-Rattle_Medicine-772.aspx

'Shamanic Dream Perspectives.' Compass Dreamwork, 16 Sept. 2014, www.compassdreamwork.com/Shamanic-dream-perspectives

'Shamanic Dreaming.' Corrosion-Doctors.org, 2022, www.corrosion-doctors.org/Dreaming%20is%20Personal/Shamanic.htm

Shamanic Drumming | Tom Magazine. tomtommag.com/2014/02/Shamanic-drumming

'Shamanism | Taking Charge of Your Health & Wellbeing.' Taking Charge of Your Health & Wellbeing, 2006, www.takingcharge.csh.umn.edu/Shamanism

'Smudging for Beginners – the Ultimate Starter Guide.' Zenluma, 12 Aug. 2020, www.zenluma.com/blog/crystals/smudging-for-beginners

'Spirit Plants (What Is a Spirit Plant and How to Find Your Spirit Plant).' Teal Swan, tealswan.com/resources/articles/spirit-plants-what-is-a-spirit-plant-and-how-to-find-your-spirit-plant-r359

'Spiritual Bath: DIY Energy Cleanse.' Balance, 5 Sept. 2020, www.balance-withus.com/blog/spiritual-bath-diy-energy-cleanse

'Sun Dance – Ritual and Ceremony of Native Americans.' Dancefacts.net, 2019,

www.dancefacts.net/dance-list/sun-dance

The. 'The Origins of Shamanism: Shamanism Beliefs & History.' Gaia, 2017,

www.gaia.com/article/how-much-do-you-know-about-Shamanism

'The Amateur Astral Travel Guide.' The New Indian Express,

www.newindianexpress.com/lifestyle/spirituality/2013/may/12/The-amateur-Astral-travel-guide-476418.html

'The Best Meditations for Having a Literal Out-Of-Body Experience.' Bustle,

www.bustle.com/life/meditations-astral-projection

'The Four Winds.' The Four Winds, 12 Apr. 2016, thefourwinds.com/blog/Shamanism/what-is-a-Shamans-mesa/.

'The Medicine Wheel.' Windspeaker.com, 2020, windspeaker.com/teachings/the-medicine-wheel

'The Purpose of Shamanic Gazing.' Parallel Perception, 16 Apr. 2012,

parallelperception.com/2012/04/16/the-purpose-of-Shamanic-gazing

'The Story of Santa Probably Stems from Mushroom-Eating Shamans.' Gaia, www.gaia.com/article/the-story-of-santa-claus-might-come-from-mushroom-eating-Shamans

'The Three Shamanic Worlds.' RoelCrabbe.com, 30 July 2019, www.roelcrabbe.com/articles-about-Shamanism/the-three-Shamanic-worlds

Vaudoise, Mallorie. 'A Ritual to Reconnect with Your Ancestors.' Spirituality & Health, 24 Nov. 2019, www.spiritualityhealth.com/articles/2019/11/24/a-ritual-to-reconnect-with-your-ancestors

'What Are Some of the Different States of Consciousness?'
Verywell Mind,

www.verywellmind.com/lesson-four-states-of-consciousness-2795293

'What Are the 7 Chakras? A Guide of the Energy Centers and
Their Effects.' Arhanta Yoga Ashram, 13 June 2019,
www.arhantayoga.org/blog/7-chakras-introduction-energy-centers-
effect

'What I Mean When I Say 'Ancestors.'' Impact Shamanism,

www.impactShamanism.com/blog/2021/4/9/what-i-mean-when-i-say-
ancestors

Made in the USA
Coppell, TX
26 April 2023

16075749R00125